TEXT ME A STRATEGY

*How to encourage students
to develop the skills they need to become
independent learners*

Kathy Paterson

Pembroke Publishers Limited

© 2009 Pembroke Publishers
538 Hood Road
Markham, Ontario, Canada L3R 3K9
www.pembrokepublishers.com

Distributed in the U.S. by Stenhouse Publishers
480 Congress Street
Portland, ME 04101
www.stenhouse.com

We acknowledge the financial support of the Government of Canada through the Book Publishing Industry Development Program (BPIDP) for our publishing activities.

We acknowledge the assistance of the Government of Ontario through the Ontario Media Development Corporation's Ontario Book Initiative.

Library and Archives Canada Cataloguing in Publication

Paterson, Kathy, 1943-
Text me a strategy : how to encourage students to develop the skills they need to become independent learners / Kathy Paterson.

Includes index.
ISBN 978-1-55138-233-3

1. Independent study. I. Title.

LB1049.P37 2009   371.39'43   C2008-907452-1

Editor: Kate Revington
Cover Design: John Zehethofer
Typesetting: Jay Tee Graphics Ltd.

Printed and bound in Canada
9 8 7 6 5 4 3 2 1

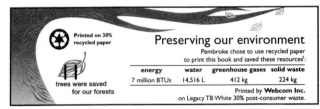

Contents

Introduction: Strategies for Independence

With the vast amount of information available on the Internet, why would anyone want yet another source for strategy instruction? The very vastness of the Internet is the reason. Time is a non-renewable resource for teachers; they want or need immediate fixes for immediate problems. This book provides those. It has taken the most effective strategies, those tested in the classroom and proven to work, and presented them according to the problems or problematic areas they best address.

Teachers don't have time to research the Internet for strategies. Nor do they have time to peruse myriad books, articles, or journals for ideas. Yet they *do* want to provide the best learning environment possible for their students. By sharing strategies with the students in their classes, they will be doing this. By keeping *Text Me a Strategy* on their desks, readily accessible, they will never be far away from a new strategy to share.

Help Students Learn for Life

Most educators want to do more than teach their students facts and formulas. They want to help their students to be successful in life. In order to do this, teachers need to adopt approaches somewhat different from the listen-and-learn one advocated by most curricula. There must be more instruction in *how* students are to do something on their own and less on doing what teachers say. There must be strategy instruction in learning, communicating, organizing, discovering, understanding, creating, and living well — the themes of this book. By helping young people find personal success with these seven essential aspects of development, teachers can facilitate their students' overall growth into happy, successful adulthood. As Ralph Waldo Emerson put it, they can help students to develop their "withins."

"What lies behind us and what lies before us are tiny matters compared to what lies within us."
— Ralph Waldo Emerson

The paradox of teaching is that good teaching makes teaching unnecessary! The essential goal of a great teacher is to make students capable of self-motivation, self-instruction, self-discovery, self-training, and ultimately, self-realization as productive adults. The teaching, practising, and reinforcing of strategies, such as those suggested in this book, will accomplish this.

Teach Explicit Strategies

A strategy, by definition, is a plan or approach, a set of related skills that make possible a certain result. In many cases, a strategy has a long-range dimension; it becomes an almost automatic action or series of actions that can be called upon to solve problems, aid memory, or assist with a variety of intellectual or social situations. In other words, an effective strategy learned in childhood can help students with lifelong learning, communicating, organizing, discovering, understanding, creating, and living well.

As adults and professionals, we use strategies daily when we skillfully carry out plans to achieve specific results. Instinctively used strategies are reflections of whatever we want achieved. We use them when we recall names, facts, numbers, and data through mnemonic devices; when we plan, organize, and collate information; when we graphically represent ideas and concepts for comprehension and clarification; and when we illuminate by sequencing, relating, or comparing.

Children, however, do not automatically make use of such strategies — they need to be taught to do so. Many of the strategies here will already be familiar — there is little that is truly "new" when it comes to teaching — but their presentation and suggestions for use may be refreshing, even novel, to instructors. Of course, there *are* innovative brand-new strategies as well, many of which were provided by students.

Although teachers have always used strategy instruction, today's almost overwhelming curricula make the need to provide this kind of self-sufficiency training even greater. It is impossible for educators — no matter how effective and efficient they may be — to *teach* all that is required for students to absorb in a given term. The best methodology is to teach *strategies* for learning, communicating, organizing, discovering, understanding, and creating, as well as generally living and growing well in our busy world.

Once during my career as a Junior High teacher, I knew that all my coaching in strategy use was having a powerful effect when I was challenged to give a strategy. The scenario is worth sharing.

We were struggling with an abstract grammar concept when the student suddenly voiced loudly: "OK! I don't get this stuff. It's driving me crazy! Teacher, couldn't you PLEASE just give us one of those strategy things to help us figure this out?"

Unfortunately, I could think of no strategy to offer and told the student so. Then another student piped up: "I know what the strategy for this is — the B-H-W strategy!" I knew I was probably going to regret it, but, of course, I asked what the B-H-W strategy was. "Boring Hard Work!" came the response.

I also recall with a smile an encounter with a Grade 7 student who was busy with her cell phone in class — a forbidden activity. When I moved to her desk, the appropriate look of displeasure on my face, she readily surrendered the phone to me. On its face was this message: "Text me a strategy for dumping my boy friend." We had been learning and using many useful strategies in class, but not one for that particular problem. It was, however, obvious that the student had internalized the value of strategies for problem solving.

Once they have been introduced to strategies and encouraged to practise and apply them, kids do remember — and use —them. Every strategy is designed for independent use; students can draw on them anytime, anywhere for the rest of their lives. In addition, the strategies offered in this book have been "named" and presented concisely for easy instruction, practice, and recall.

Why the Names Matter

Strategy names have been derived in a number of ways. The name may be a word spelled out as an acronym (e.g., PUP, a strategy related to emotions); a series of letters, numbers, or a combination of both that relate directly to the steps in the strategy (e.g., D-R-T-A, a comprehension strategy); a metaphor (e.g., B-B [Building Blocks] strategy for writing); or a special mnemonic where the first letter of each word helps recall the strategy steps, as in CALM, a strategy for helping others in need.

Why is this strategy naming important? In order to be memorable, something must first catch our attention. This understanding is the premise on which this book is based. I *know* that the teaching of named strategies works. There are three important reasons for the names.

- One, they allow for rapid recall or retrieval.
- Two, they facilitate teaching and discussion of specific strategies as needed.
- Three, they are quirky and "funky" and thus appeal to kids of all ages.

One incident that I always recall with a smile demonstrates the value of naming. A boy in Grade 3 was having a terrible day. His frustration had escalated until he was close to that critical point of no return. Suddenly, he shouted, "Teacher! I need a P-T-O right now!" A P-T-O is a Personal Time Out (see page 104) and the student not only knew the strategy by name, but also identified the perfect time to use it.

Perhaps the best thing about the strategy names is that they resemble the text-messaging codes and abbreviations with which today's kids are so comfortable. Think of how readily we now recognize *lol, TLC, PS,* or *FYI.* Kids are so quick to use this form of text "code" that they almost immediately file into their long-term memories the names of those strategies they find most useful. No doubt, the students will remember and use the strategies by name more easily than their teachers.

Most of these strategies will work as well in adulthood as in childhood so the catchy names will simplify and facilitate long-term strategy retrieval. However, even if the names are forgotten, that doesn't mean the strategies, the steps leading to positive outcomes, will be lost. The most effective ones will be remembered forever!

Take the Choose and Use Approach

Naturally, not *all* of the strategies offered will be used by *all* of the students; nor should they be. Introducing too many strategies at once can lead to confusion. Strategies are best taught or used on a need-to-know or a desire-to-motivate basis. When students need to know how to proceed, how to better understand their world, or how to learn independently, there are strategies to help. When kids are bored, restless, or unmotivated, sharing of a novel strategy with a catchy name may be just the thing to "turn them on." Teachers can choose those most useful for meeting the specific needs of their students, share them, and then watch their charges develop autonomously.

Often, several strategies are suggested for the same problem or situation, so the Choose and Use idea becomes critical. Not only will teachers choose and use those strategies most relevant to specific situations, but students, too, will be encouraged to choose and use. Certain strategies will appeal to some kids; others will appeal to different kids. In other words, the more strategies we teach our students, the better prepared they will be to independently use their favorites.

Students will choose and use strategies they have discovered through practice and think work for them; not all will make the same choices.

As I see it, teachers are responsible for encouraging application of the Choose and Use approach whenever a student is faced with a new, potentially troublesome, or even just thought-provoking situation. The idea is to provide students with an array of readily usable strategies that will work at any grade or age and will carry on into later life.

Thus, the paradox: teachers *seemingly* making teaching redundant.

Happily for us, effective teachers only *seem* to eliminate the need for their role. Teachers will forever be needed as they are models, leaders, facilitators, and supporters of the children whose evolution into self-sufficient adults they are assisting. The more teachers fulfill these roles, the more children grow and learn.

Internalizing Strategies

This book offers more than 100 strategies and these are only a small representation of those used by teachers everywhere. Realistically, do we expect our students to use and remember them all? Of course not! Our goal as teachers is to help kids think and work things out on their own. So, if they use even *some* of the steps of a strategy to meet an objective, but forget the strategy's name, it doesn't matter. The strategy names and simple, sequenced steps are for teaching, initial learning, recalling, and reinforcement purposes. Once a strategy has become internalized, a student will be able to bring it to mind and use it, or part of it, as needed. That is what makes the strategy authentic or real — and what makes strategy instruction so important.

I'm sure you will find that you regularly use many of the strategies. I frequently follow the steps involved with most of them, but seldom recollect their names. It's how, when, and why a strategy is employed that makes it significant. However, don't overlook the effectiveness of sharing the text-type, catchy, and kid-motivating names when introducing and practising the strategies.

With this in mind, I caution against "testing" students on strategies. Instead of expecting kids to recall names and list steps, watch for the more intrinsic *use* of strategies at appropriate times or places. Pay attention to how students take advantage of strategies in context or to when they struggle and may benefit from a particular strategy. When you remind kids that a particular strategy may be useful, however, allow them freedom with use of the steps. Remember: Whatever works for them is what counts. The reality of strategy instruction is that it should help students live successfully on their own.

A Focus on Problem Solving

Every strategy addresses a problem within one of seven critical areas: learning, communicating, organizing, discovering, understanding, creating, and living well. However, it should be noted that the strategies often pertain to more than one area. They can be used whenever and wherever the students need them. Their focus on procedures, plans, and processes — not just outcomes — helps makes them valuable.

Every strategy follows the same three-part format related to the problem.

1. *Purpose:* How does the strategy address the problem?
2. *Strategy Display:* How does the strategy work? In other words, what form does it take?
   This section is written to help teachers present the strategy in the manner most easily remembered by students.
3. *Quick Tips:* What specific teaching tips accompany each strategy?
   This section provides teachers with information and motivational guidelines to use during strategy instruction.

Good practice is to locate a strategy to teach or share according to a problem or difficulty that students face now or are likely to encounter. If more than one strategy is offered for a single situation, I recommend giving students a choice.

Build a Strategy Base

All strategies require similar basic instruction. Each needs to be introduced by explaining its name, purpose, and application. After the introduction and modelling of a strategy, students are given immediate practice in it. From that time on, teachers should refer to the strategy by name and remind students of good times to employ it. This constant prompting serves as both reinforcement and relearning for the particular strategy; it is an important stage in the process.

Seven steps to follow when carrying out strategy instruction are outlined below.

1. Introduce the strategy by name, pointing out why it was given that name.
2. Model strategy use.
3. Outline the steps or stages both visually and verbally; model again if necessary.
4. Create a chart or individual pages that briefly explain the strategy.
5. Practise together, withdrawing your assistance as students become more proficient.
6. Encourage students to use a strategy independently.
7. Regularly remind students where or when a strategy may be useful.

I like mounting an outline of a strategy on a wall chart or on the chalkboard until students are familiar with it, usually about a week. Sometimes, I reserve a particular bulletin board for several strategies, changing them weekly or as needed. On this same board is a continually growing list of learned-strategy names.

Some teachers choose to provide each student with a Strategy Book in which taught strategies are recorded for future independent reference. Kids seem to like this accumulation of handy and useful approaches to solving problems, all named in interesting text-messaging ways that appeal to them. In any event, it is important to give students some kind of strategy base to deal with the challenges of their lives.

1

Remembering to Learn

Learning is a complex mental function that leads to the development of the human being. The goal of teaching, it refers to the act of becoming skilled at or gaining knowledge in. It implies remembering — and for the purposes of this book, the area of memory will be given focus. Remembering is the ability to store, retain, and retrieve information. I am making the assumption that in order to learn, one must remember and that good teaching can, and should, provide strategies to enhance memory.

In order for learning to occur, there must be direction, modelling, practice, and reinforcement. Here, I am simplifying learning into examination of specific strategies for specific problems teachers and students face in the classroom. There are myriad sources and resources for training and enhancing memory. This book does not offer to *train* memory so much as to provide simple strategies that will work on a daily basis regardless of age, gender, socio-economic class, or intellectual ability. It particularly suggests strategies for students to use when reviewing or studying on their own.

We are all familiar with *instant* memory-enhancing ploys, those little "games" that help us recall facts as they are presented. As adults, we use them almost automatically. How often, for instance, do you use a mnemonic to help remember the name of a new acquaintance or a password for an Internet account? This book includes some strategies you will find familiar.

Strategies of this nature are examples of formal learning procedures, planning processes that help with information retention and retrieval, and are realized through teacher–student relationships. I refer to these as learning strategies. Areas addressed in this chapter include

- getting focused
- studying and reviewing
- committing to memory
- retrieving information
- learning a procedure

Getting Focused

Problem: **Kids often "zone out," intentionally or not, when presented with a new learning or when reviewing or studying previously "learned" material. There is a lack of focus on the material to be received.**

FACE

Focus
Actively
Compute
Enter

This strategy was created by a computer literate Grade 4 student.

Purpose: The FACE strategy prompts students to maintain focus and purposefully "place" the new information in their memories.

Strategy Display

Focus attention fully on what is being read, said, or shown.
Actively remove distractions from your mind by telling yourself to pay attention.
Compute or process the information as it is provided. Make sure you understand it. Even it it's as simple as a phone number or as complicated as a scientific formula, you must sort out any problem areas and clarify them. Do not go on if you don't understand!
Enter the information into your short-term memory by repeating it several times or taking whatever action(s) you think would work for you.

Quick Tips

- Introduce the strategy by name drawing attention to the "authentic" meaning of the acronym as well as the "new" meaning. "When you're using FACE to help you remember, you will be using your *face*." You may want to brainstorm what working hard to remember looks like: perhaps furrowed brow, closed eyes or eyes looking up, and lip biting.
- Discuss the idea of actively removing distractions. Brainstorm for ways to do this, such as giving the head a shake, telling yourself you will think about something later, or visualizing a Stop sign when your mind starts to wander.
- Note that when someone pushes "Enter" on a computer, the material is placed in memory. Point out how students can follow a similar operation with their brains.
- Discuss how the FACE strategy is like using a computer.

G-R-T-R

Purpose: The G-R-T-R strategy reminds kids that they have to prepare themselves to learn and provides steps for them to do this.

Get
Ready
To
Remember

Strategy Display

1. Begin by removing distractions from the surrounding area (desk, table, hands, and vision).
2. Now, relax and take two deep breaths, holding each for five seconds, and then exhaling by blowing out through the mouth.
3. During the deep breathing, close your eyes. Empty your mind by visualizing a black curtain or wall.
4. Open your eyes and concentrate (focus) on the topic to be presented, read, or absorbed.

If your mind starts to wander, use the Stop strategy (next in this book) to refocus.

Quick Tips

- Discuss the problems kids face when they are trying to learn something new, but can't seem to pay attention; their minds wander to topics they find more interesting.
- Practise the deep breathing and black curtain focusing exercise.
- Discuss distractions. These can be as small as a bracelet on the wrist or as big as a stimulating poster in direct line of sight. Some kids are able to mentally remove distractions; others need to physically remove them.

- Often, just drawing the idea of distractions to their attention is sufficient to downplay this form of interruption to thinking.

STOP

Purpose: This quick strategy helps kids to refocus when they experience wandering minds.

Strategy Display

1. As soon as you realize your mind is wandering (e.g., you have read a page and have no idea what was on it), close your eyes and visualize a big Stop sign.
2. Stare at the sign in your mind's eye for about 10 seconds; tell yourself to stop thinking about what was off task.
3. Tell yourself you will think about the distracting idea later. By giving yourself permission to think of it later, you will have a better chance of not thinking of it now.

Quick Tips

- Discuss the purpose of a Stop sign.
- Invite kids to close their eyes and visualize a Stop sign.
- Discuss the problem of wandering minds, especially during reading or lectures.
- Practise the Stop strategy together. Invite the students to think about their favorite book or television show while you provide them with some specific information. Let their minds wander for a few seconds and then begin your "lecture." Students will be responsible for activating the Stop strategy and letting you know at what point they do this. For example, they might raise a finger or hand when they are fully focused on your words.

Studying and Reviewing

Problem: **Some kids are great when it comes to learning and retaining information while in school, but when faced with independent study, they fall short. They don't seem to have the necessary study skills to make their time efficient and effective.**

S-Q-4R

Purpose: This strategy, one of the oldest presented here and likely familiar to all teachers, provides a framework primarily for study purposes.

Survey
Question
Read
Recite
Review
Reflect

Strategy Display

Survey: Quickly skim the material, giving attention to general content, headings, titles, illustrations, and charts.
Question: Formulate questions based on the headings, subtitles, and so on.
Read: Read the section and try to answer all your questions.
Recite: Talk about or speak the answers out loud.

Review: Reread the material, paying close attention to summaries or to parts you didn't understand the first time. If you still don't understand, ask more questions.

Reflect: Take a few moments to close your eyes and think about the material.

Quick Tips

- Discuss problems with independent studying.
- Practise asking good questions pertaining to titles, headings, and illustrations. Questions could be based on Bloom's taxonomy of questions: consider the categories of knowledge, comprehension, application, analysis, synthesis, and evaluation. Answer the questions after reading.
- Practise asking questions based on areas not understood. The practice of asking and answering oneself aids comprehension.
- Practise the S-Q-4R steps together.

R-W-C-S-R

Read
Write
Cover
Say
Review

You can recall the letter sequence with the following mnemonic:

Real Women Can Sing Rap.

It's interesting how often boys change the "can" to "can't." No matter — they still remember the sequence.

Purpose: The R-W-C-S-R strategy reminds kids of a good sequence to follow when trying to review and study material.

Strategy Display

Read over a part or chunk the material to be studied or reviewed.
Write quick notes of the key words, ideas, and concepts.
Cover what you have written and recall it mentally.
Say to yourself, using memory, the key notes you have written.
Review by uncovering the notes and confirming what you have recalled.

Quick Tips

- Discuss the importance of using a strategy such as R-W-C-S-R to help with studying.
- Discuss the mnemonic for recalling the initial letters. (If kids don't like the mnemonic, invite them to create their own.)
- Practise R-W-C-S-R together.

ASPIRE

Approach
Select
Piece
Investigate
Review
Evaluate

Purpose: The familiar ASPIRE strategy provides a learning format for students, thus helping them remember material.

Strategy Display

Approach the work with a positive attitude.
Select a reasonable chunk of material to cover or study.
Piece together what you've learned; do this at regular intervals, determined either by time or chunking of material.
Investigate anything you don't understand. Seek help if you are unable to comprehend it alone.
Review the content.
Evaluate your progress. Determine whether you need additional study on this content or not.

Quick Tips

- Discuss the difficulties involved with trying to remember content.
- Invite students to share approaches to learning content that have been successful or unsuccessful for them.
- When introducing the ASPIRE strategy, draw attention to the literal meaning of the word "aspire." Practise the strategy together.

Committing to Memory

Problem: **Some students have more difficulty learning material than others. If they fail to see the relevance or significance of what they are supposed to be learning, it may be impossible for them to remember it.**

DOUBLE-M

Purpose: The Double-M strategy helps students to attach authentic meaning to new information. This "linking" strategy facilitates learning and remembering.

Make
Meaning

Strategy Display

1. Read or listen to material while trying to fit it into your own life and experiences. For example: If the new information is historical, think about how your life has been affected by these events; if the new material is a math formula, think how this specific formula might affect your life.
2. If you are unable to find a meaningful relationship, seek assistance from peers or teacher, or try projecting the concept into your future. How might the material relate to you then?

Quick Tips

- Ask students what makes learning or remembering difficult. Try to draw out the idea that "it is not interesting or real to them."
- Discuss how to make material more real by attaching it to something in their lives.
- Practise doing this with single statements, such as the following.
  The formula for the area of a square: They might have to buy a rug for their bedrooms.
  Information about scientific elements: They might have to know what is in a cleaning solution.
  Information about trees and forests: They might have to know which wood would make a good camp fire.
  Information about grammar: They might have to write a letter of introduction for a job.

Problem: **Often, there is more information about a topic than students can recall: they feel overwhelmed by the amount of material. They may remember only sketchy points and be missing chunks of relevant information. Sometimes the "wrong" information is remembered: the irrelevant facts that, in retrospect, are unimportant. Kids will focus on reams of extraneous details about a topic and miss the big picture. Some feel the need to remember everything in order to be good students and end up remembering little.**

LINK

Purpose: The LINK strategy teaches students to tie together, or link, important and similar facts during the memory process.

Strategy Display

Look at or attend to the new information.
Interpret it by thinking of how it fits with information you already know.
Notice the similarities and mentally link them or put them together.
Keep the new and old information together in your mind. If you continue to "add" new information to old or already existing information, the new material will be easier to understand and recall.

Quick Tips

- Discuss how we use computers to "add" or link new information to old by moving the cursor and inserting similar information beside what is already there.
- Discuss doing this procedure mentally.
- Practise by providing some facts about what has been studied in the past and discussing where they can link these facts in their minds.

KISS

Purpose: Simple material is easiest to remember. The KISS strategy teaches kids to split complex material into simpler components for easier understanding and memorization. This activity, sometimes referred to as "chunking," seems easier for kids to remember through the KISS name.

Strategy Display

1. Quickly scan the amount of material to be covered (read, listened to, viewed).
2. Consider your time frame. How long will you spend on this activity?
3. Divide the time into smaller units; 5 or 10 minute units are good.
4. Divide the material into chunks, or simple units, according to the number of time periods you have.
5. Spend only the allotted time on a chunk; then, in point form, summarize that section, even if you haven't quite finished it. Use only key words in your summaries.
6. Complete all the simple summaries in the predetermined time periods.

Quick Tips

- Begin by reassuring kids that they don't always have to "read or listen to every word" or scrutinize every detail of a visual representation.
- Discuss, teach, or review chunking: dividing text according to manageable pieces, defined by such things as headings, paragraphs, and obvious sections.
- Practise skimming to decide where to chunk.

- A good practice run is to provide several pages of text to be read in a 15-minute frame. You can have the text already divided into chunks (defined by lines) and have key words in each chunk highlighted.
- This strategy is so important that lots of practice is warranted. You will want students to become very familiar with it.

ISIN

I
See
It
Now

Purpose: ISIN reminds kids to "see it" or use visualization while trying to remember facts. It is a "think color, shape, and texture" strategy.

Strategy Display

1. Read or listen to the information while mentally making a picture related to the information.
2. Close your eyes and really "see" the visualization you have made.
3. With your eyes still closed, recall as many of the facts as you can while still focusing on the mind picture.

Quick Tips

- Begin with a discussion about how we create pictures in the mind. You might have students close their eyes and ask them to visualize a particularly graphic scene as you describe it.
- Move to discussion of how to attach a mind picture to some piece of information they are trying to remember. For example, if trying to recall a particular formula for science or mathematics, they could visualize the components as little "characters" interacting according to the principle or themselves as "actors" in the procedure. For instance, for $E = mc^2$ students see themselves as "Energetic because of eating 2 McDonald's burgers."
- Remind students the visualization can be nonsense; it simply has to fit with whatever is being learned.
- Remind students to revisit the mind picture when they next need to recall the information.
- Do a few visualizations together so they can get the idea. Here are a few suggestions:

  - The grammar rule "when two vowels go out walking, the first one usually does the talking": Perhaps visualize O and A as little walking characters, with O being the biggest and in front, and telling A what to do, as with a younger sibling.
  - An isosceles triangle, which has two equal sides/angles, one different: Perhaps visualize a long icicle hanging from a roof.

Problem: **Some people forget information as quickly as it is given. A good example is names. Trying to recall the name of a person, place, or even thing can be enough to drive one crazy. Similarly, some of us can't remember a simple math or science concept as soon as the instruction is over. It's hard for many kids (and many adults) to recall information when it is presented and received only through speaking and listening.**

MOVE-IT

Move
It

Although it obviously can't be used all the time, this walk-and-talk approach really works for tough-to-recall facts.

Purpose: The Move-It strategy encourages whole body involvement in the learning and memorization process. It is based on the knowledge that the greater the physical involvement, the greater the learning will be.

Strategy Display

1. When faced with a difficult concept involving memorization, perhaps the spelling of a tough word or the way to do long division, find a way to *physically* demonstrate the idea.

    For example, if trying to remember somewhat difficult words, such as "column," "embarrass," or "liaison," draw them in the air, stand up and walk around while thinking quietly about the spellings, or with eyes closed, shake your hands in the air — one shake for each letter — while visualizing the letters.

    As another example, when trying to memorize important dates or the Periodic Table of the Elements, stand up, and as you say each fact aloud and aim to commit it to memory, click fingers, stamp feet, clap, or do some other action. This may seem silly, but it works! Creativity helps.

2. When you have done it once, wait for a few minutes, then repeat the physical movement; note how this helps to recall the mental information.

Quick Tips

- Discuss what kinds of information kids have the most trouble remembering.
- Invite them to think of physical movements that they could make while trying to put the information into memory. Encourage big and small movements. Brainstorm physical movements: clapping, tapping, clicking, air-writing, marching, shaking fingers or hands, arm circling, and touching nose or toes among them.
- Discuss how the brainstormed movements could help with memorization and then practise doing so with new facts.
- Point out that the Move-It strategy is best used when working at home trying to put information into long-term memory.

WIN

Write
It
Now

Whether done with pen, pencil, or finger, writing things down really works. I do this all the time to remember peoples' names.

Purpose: The WIN strategy reminds kids to write something just learned. The perceptual-motor connections promote remembering.

Strategy Display

1. As soon as possible after a new name, word, or concept is introduced, write it down on whatever is available. If no paper and pencil are handy, write it on your hand using a finger.
2. Within the next 5 to 10 minutes, revisit what you wrote (even if it was on your hand).

Quick Tips

- Discuss the importance of remembering names. Ask who has had the problem of forgetting the name of someone to whom they have been introduced. Ask, too, whether anyone has forgotten a name or term that came up in science or history.
- Brainstorm all the possible ways of "writing it down" (e.g., notes, memos, scrap paper, imaginary writing in the air, on arm, or hand).
- Practise with a few imaginary words.

T-RT

Test
Re-Test

Purpose: The T-RT (Test Re-Test) strategy provides a plan that leads to consistent success with spelling development. Sometimes called the "Five Day Plan," it is a familiar strategy for learning spelling words.

Strategy Display

The steps are very specific; they must be followed exactly as presented.

See the line master on page 20.

Quick Tips

- Allow only about 10 minutes a day for these activities, preferably the same 10 minutes each day. For example, you might choose the time just before recess.
- Change the partners weekly.
- If at first some kids choose words that are too easy, allow this but aim to generally shape their behavior(s) so that they begin to include more difficult words on their lists. (Usually, this happens automatically as they start to see the benefits of the T-RT strategy.)

In addition to personal words, there is a great deal of incidental learning of the words partners have chosen.

- It may be helpful to have ready some suggestions for Wednesday's study time. A few ideas follow.

  - Using the words you spelled incorrectly, reorder all the letters in each word and see how many other smaller words you can find within each word. (This activity promotes close examination of words.)
  - Use the words you both got wrong to write *one* good sentence using them all.
  - No words wrong? Pick a few of the toughest and find out more about them, for example, how to make them plural, what prefixes work with them, and their etymology. (Encourage these students to choose more difficult words next week.)

Problem: All too often, students move on from learning something as soon as they believe they have mastered it. They fail to see the value in "over-learning" — a technique that prompts material to move from short- to long-term memory — and consequently, not be quickly forgotten.

GRRRR

Get
Repeating
Repeating
Repeating
Repeating

Purpose: The GRRR strategy comically reminds kids to repeat the learning many times, even after they feel they know it cold. Repetition is one of the best ways to promote remembering, and although we modern-day teachers may feel we don't use anything as basic as that, it can be useful.

Test Re-Test, or the Five Day Plan

Monday: Create your own individual word list (about 8 to 10 words) based on previous errors, interest, and need. Your teacher then adds one to four words, choice based on group errors, thematic content, and core subjects. Lists are handed in, the teacher does a quick check (to be sure all are spelled correctly), and returns lists by Tuesday.

Tuesday: Work with a partner — you'll work with the same partner all week. One at a time, give each other your personal lists as a pre-test. Correct both lists together. You correct your partner's list; your partner corrects yours.

Wednesday: With your partners or with a small group, review the lists and "play" with the words from the lists, paying attention to any mistakes from pre-tests. One way of playing is to ask your partner to use words that were misspelled in sentences about a topic you choose.

Thursday: Test each other again, mark the tests together, and study only the words you misspelled. Prompt your partner to spell any missed words again. Review, study, and learn the correct spellings together. You may want to chant the words out loud or write them down. Use whatever method works best for you.

Friday: Give your partner a final test; your partner will give you yours. Hand the tests in to the teacher for final grading and recording of marks. Any words still spelled incorrectly are moved to next week's list.

Strategy Display

1. Read the material to be remembered out loud.
2. Repeat the reading silently this time (first repeat).
3. Close your eyes and *repeat* the information by mentally recalling as much as possible (second repeat).
4. Open your eyes and repeat the reading silently again, paying particular attention to anything important you might have missed on the second repeat (third repeat).
5. Without looking at the text, write down the information (fourth repeat).

Quick Tips

- Begin by discussing the implication of "grrrr." (It might be the way you feel when you can't remember something you just learned.)
- Provide a nonsense rhyme or something short, such as a limerick, that the class will learn by using the GRRR strategy.
- Point out how this strategy is also useful for spelling words.
- Suggest that additional "Rs," or repetitions, could be added, if necessary, to succeed in remembering.

Problem: **Not all memory material comes from the written word. Often, it is necessary to learn and remember graphic detail, such as maps, anatomy, and scientific diagrams. Students trying to memorize pictures or illustrations may experience more difficulty with this than they would with textual material.**

VIS-CLOZE

VISual
Cloze

Purpose: The VIS-Cloze strategy encourages students to remember graphics by "deleting" sections and mentally filling in the blanks much as is done with other types of cloze activities (filling in blanks, completing open-ended sentences).

Strategy Display

1. Stare at the graphic and look at all the main components.
2. Copy the graphic and intentionally leave part of it missing OR cover part of the graphic with paper.
3. Visualize the missing parts, using what's visible as clues for what's not visible.
4. Repeat the process, changing the "missing" parts.

Quick Tips

- Discuss areas of study where kids are required to remember graphics. (These may include studies of maps and anatomy.)
- Do a few sentence clozes together (At school we l - - - n.). Point out how the rest of the sentence helps figure out what is missing.
- Draw parallels between this type of cloze activity and the VIS-Cloze strategy, pointing out how they can use what's there on a graphic to determine what's not there.

Retrieving Information

Problem: Even after a fact has been "memorized," it can sometimes be difficult to retrieve. This "It's-on-the-tip-of-my-tongue" feeling is something we have all experienced. Kids experience that too, and it can be very frustrating.

ABC+

This strategy does not work for recall of numbers or formulas.

Purpose: The ABC+ strategy makes use of the sequenced letters of the alphabet to help "jog" name or fact retrieval.

Strategy Display

1. Can't remember a fact? a name? Begin with the letter "A" and say the sound of the letter to yourself — *ahh* — while thinking about what you are trying to retrieve.
2. If this doesn't trigger a response, continue with each letter of the alphabet in sequence.

If you haven't remembered the first time through, a second time probably won't help either. This is a one-shot strategy, but the frequency with which it does work is amazing.

Quick Tips

My husband always uses this strategy to recall names and swears by its usefulness. I figure if an "old man" can use it so well, surely our students can do the same.

- Quickly model the strategy by saying you are trying to remember the name of a person to whom you were recently introduced. You can see the person's face in your mind, but the name escapes you. Say the sounds of the letters as opposed to their names *ahh, buh, cuh* . . . When you get to *mmm*, quickly say "Mary."

PZ-IT

Personalize-It

Purpose: The PZ-It strategy encourages kids to make a new learning relevant by personalizing it. They attach authentic meaning to the learning so that it can be more easily retrieved when the tip-of-the-tongue syndrome occurs.

Strategy Display

1. Carefully examine what is being learned, perhaps general information, specific formulas, or sequenced facts.
2. Find a way to "attach" it to something you already know, either real or imaginary.

   Example: Information about the planets in our solar system
   Personalize-It: Think of a book or movie about space you have recently seen. Imagine you are in the book, movie, or story and are visiting the planets.

3. Next time you are trying to recall the fact(s) and are "stuck," think of the personal connections you made.

Quick Tips

- This strategy may be difficult for some kids until they grasp the idea of "attaching" new knowledge to old. Help can be in the form of leading questions that shape their thinking towards what you know they already know.

- Invite them to think of something they already know about a topic before introducing new information. Explain that the goal is to personalize the information, to make it "individual." Discuss how different people have different knowledge bases so that how one student personalizes new information may be different from how another does this. Consequently, it is an individual task.

Learning a Procedure

Problem: **The whole idea of learning a new procedure fills some kids with anxiety or a sense of not being capable. (Compare this to the way most adults feel when faced with "assembling" a piece of furniture or child's toy, and having to follow instructions to do so.)**

LEARN

Purpose: The LEARN strategy provides a sequence of steps for learning and executing a procedure. By employing the LEARN strategy, kids will feel less anxious and better able to continue.

Strategy Display

Look
Evaluate
Ask
Review
Note

Look at the information provided. Skim it to get the general idea of what's to be done or what's to come.
Evaluate the directions or information to see if it's written in a way you can understand. If it is, move to the Review step; if it's not, move to the next step.
Ask for help before beginning, or try to find an alternative source of information.
Review your progress as you go — don't wait until the end to discover an early mistake that makes a big difference to the result.
Note, once finished, any difficulties you may have had and recheck to see if you handled them correctly. If not, you may need to return to the third step: Ask.

Quick Tips

- The LEARN strategy works well when kids are given a set of directions to follow, for example, to carry out an experiment in science, assemble something in woodworking, or even follow the directions for writing a proper essay. It breaks down their use of directions into manageable units and prevents escalating errors.
- Discuss the difficulties with following written directions. (Ask if any of their parents have had to put together a piece of furniture.)
- Show kids how to evaluate the directions before they start manipulating the variables. Taking this proactive step often prevents frustration later.
- Talk about the LEARN strategy and tie its name to the fact that they are learning to learn when using it.

2

Communicating

Communicating is transmitting or passing on information or feelings. It implies a common understanding of language and methodology between persons. It is a life skill. Communicating effectively, however, is difficult for many people, not just for our students. Because it involves the assigning of meaning and happens at many levels between sender and receiver, there are myriad ways for communication to break down. This is where teaching strategies for better "message transfer" helps to increase the accuracy, ease, and efficiency of communication.

In education, communication refers largely to writing, listening, and speaking skills, with most of the in-class time usually spent on these areas. As teachers we are concerned with our students' abilities to write concisely and correctly, to speak clearly, and to listen actively. We cannot assume they all have innate abilities to do any or all of these. It is true that we "communicate to get our needs met." Thus it holds true that if kids have difficulty communicating, at least some of their needs are not being met. We can also safely assume that weak communication skills in school will carry on to be weak communication skills in adulthood. Let's try to protect our students from that as much as possible.

The communication strategies offered in this book will help students do a better job of getting their needs met and improve both their written and oral communication. The underlying assumption is that a quick strategy just might prevent further problems. By addressing problems with communicating in school, teachers will be providing students with strategies that will always serve them well.

Areas addressed in this chapter include

- speaking in public and in conversation
- making effective oral and written presentations of ideas
- listening actively
- communicating with persuasive intent
- listening with compassion
- responding orally and in writing
- exploring clear and interesting voice cadence
- dealing with unmotivated or apathetic writers
- getting started in writing communication
- following the conventions of good writing

Public Speaking and Talking

Problem: **When speaking either formally or informally, students have difficulty getting the point across as they talk around the topic; they are unable to be concise and precise.**

S-A-S

Purpose: The S-A-S strategy reminds kids to hone material, to keep what they want to say short and sweet.

Strategy Display

1. Before speaking, take the necessary time (perhaps only a few seconds) to think what you really want to say. In other words, avoid rushing into the conversation or report without prior thought.
2. Think specifics — consciously remove irrelevant material or unnecessary facts. Stick to the point.
3. Especially if you are getting ready to deliver a formal report, practise out loud.
4. If you find yourself rambling, stop, breathe, and mentally cut unnecessary words.

Quick Tips

- Discuss the problem of rambling when talking. Draw from kids their personal experiences with this type of talk and how it has affected them as listeners.
- Discuss how the S-A-S strategy makes it easier to listen to what another person has to say.
- Present a rambling, wordy speech that you have prepared, and together with the class, examine it. Apply S-A-S, and then invite a student to present the revised content.
- Discuss why the revised presentation is better — more interesting, punchier, and easier for drawing out the key facts.

Problem: When getting ready to do an oral presentation of any nature, kids often feel anxious, timid, or uncomfortable. This form of communication can be very intimidating.

PREP

Purpose: PREP lessens anxiety by encapsulating the basic groundwork needed for a successful communication.

Strategy Display

Prepare. Do the homework. Make a written plan of what you want to say, what you already know about the topic, and what you need to find out.
Repair — or change — areas that don't feel right, once you have practised the talk.
Engage or hook your audience right at the start. Think of a way.
Present with confidence, knowing you have followed the PREP strategy.

Quick Tips

- Discuss the meaning of "prep," as in to prep for something, and tie to the PREP strategy.
- Teach students to focus on what they *know* and to express themselves in terms of information, observations, and specifics about which they are

familiar. (It will sound more convincing than making assumptions, and they will be more confident when presenting.)

- Discuss hooks. Have kids brainstorm ideas for hooks, including these:

  asking a pertinent question
  starting with an anecdote, joke, or thought-provoking statement
  sharing a personal story or self-disclosure
  starting with a few lines of pertinent poetry or a related quotation from a famous person

- Discuss the important of the Repair step in the PREP strategy. Suggest an audience, perhaps a parent or peer.

Problem: **Sometimes in a discussion, kids repeat what another has just said, over and over again, as if they lack original ideas of their own. (Adults do this, too — it can be very annoying.) This form of communication can be frustrating for everyone involved.**

PIGGYBACK

Purpose: The Piggyback strategy shows kids how to respond to what another has said without repeating the words back or saying the same thing over and over again, while still showing what has been learned from the other speaker.

Strategy Display

1. Listen carefully to what is being said.
2. Think of what you have learned or are learning from the speaker's words.
3. Avoid saying these exact words again. Instead, piggyback what was said: put your words on top of the already spoken words — expand what was already said.

   Speaker: There are too many people in the world right now.
   You: Do you think the world is overpopulated?
   Or — and this option is better
   You: I agree that the world is overpopulated, but I don't think anything can be done about it. I read that . . .

In the second sentence, you have piggybacked what the other person said, adding something to it, and acknowledging the original words.

Quick Tips

- Discuss the Piggyback strategy by inviting kids to think of when they have played piggyback with a parent or friend. They were, in fact, adding their bodies to someone else's. Piggybacking in speech is a technique where words or ideas are "added to" something without changing the original ideas. Think again of the metaphor of riding piggyback. The person doing the carrying does not *change*. Similarly, the ideas presented by the listener are not "changed" — they are expansions.
- Keep thinking of "adding" more words or thoughts — of piggybacking or expanding what has been said or learned — as opposed to restating the same thing.

- Model the Piggyback strategy (as a form of paraphrasing and adding to) by asking kids an open-ended question and then piggybacking a comeback to their responses.

Problem: **Some kids talk with "marbles in their mouths." They slur words, stammer, or enunciate poorly. Clear speaking is a communication survival skill that everyone needs to master.**

MIRROR, MIRROR

Mirror, Mirror

Purpose: The Mirror, Mirror strategy encourages kids to practise any important talk *in front of* a mirror, where they can read their own lips and *see* what is being said. It reminds students of the importance of speaking clearly all the time.

Strategy Display

1. Stand or sit in front of a mirror.
2. Speak or read the passage while watching your lips. Could you read your lips? If not, exaggerate the enunciation until your mouth is clearly shaping each word.
3. Continue until you see a noticeable difference in the action of your mouth.

Quick Tips

Keep the discussion non-threatening, especially if you have kids with speech impediments. Use cartoon characters or fictional characters as examples.

- Discuss the importance of clear speaking. Consider instances when there have been misunderstandings because of unclear speech.
- Discuss TV shows or movies where something a character said was missed because of "marbles in the mouth" or interfering background noise.
- Model unclear, then clear presentation of a passage, either while reading or telling.
- If possible, have small hand mirrors in class and invite students to speak clearly while watching themselves in these.

Problem: **Some people are "boring" to listen to. Their oral communication is flat, monotonous, and uninteresting and consequently fails to attract and maintain attention.**

SINGSEN

Singing
Sentence

Purpose: The SingSen strategy encourages kids to make their oral speech "flow," just like an engaging melody, with appropriate pauses throughout.

Strategy Display

1. Locate a simple reading passage.
2. Read it silently to determine sentence type and length.
3. Practise reading it aloud with fluency and flow, aware that each sentence has its own rhythm and beat, like a song.
4. Reread it aloud again, moving easily from one sentence to the next with appropriate stopping, starting, and phrasing, almost as if you are "singing" the sentences.

Quick Tips

- Discuss how a song has a flow, a rise and fall in cadence, as well as appropriate pauses after phrases or lines.
- Demonstrate reading or speaking *without* this flow — spastic and jerky — and with inappropriate pausing, such as in the middle of an obvious phrase, or without any pausing at all.
- Demonstrate reading or speaking with flow or fluency and appropriate pausing.
- Invite kids to read a sentence and exaggerate its rhythm and beat, then reread it with interesting, but not exaggerated rhythm and beat as well as appropriate pauses
- Remind kids that before giving a speech or reading aloud, they could use the SingSen strategy to prepare.

S-C-4E

Speed
Clarity
Emphasis Enthusiasm Energy Eye

Purpose: The S-C-4E strategy reminds kids of the most important qualities of a voice presentation — those traits that will make the audience want to pay attention.

Strategy Display

Practise your presentation (report, poem, speech, or argument), while paying attention to each of the S-C-4E points.

Speed: Speak briskly, but not too fast that your words slur together. A brisk pace is more interesting than a slow one.

Clarity: Each word must be clear and properly pronounced, with the accent on the correct syllable. Use proper articulation.

Emphasis: Determine the most important part of each sentence or section and put emphasis on that by speaking louder or more slowly at that point.

Enthusiasm: Be eager to speak. Showing enthusiasm for the topic makes the audience interested.

Energy: Be energetic while speaking. Even if you feel tired or restless, act focused and filled with energy for the topic. Stand tall, shoulders back, head high. (Think "chin parallel to the floor.")

Eye contact: Look from one person's eyes to another person's. Make the audience members feel like they are a part of your presentation. If you have to look at notes, pause, refer to them, and then renew your eye contact.

Quick Tips

- Demonstrate both a good and a bad oral presentation for the kids.
- Invite them to critique both.
- Review and practise S-C-4E together, then invite students to begin preparing for oral presentations of their choice.

Problem: **Today's kids constantly have to leave voice messages and too often these messages are incomplete or even baffling to the receivers.**

3W-NO.

Who What When
Number

Purpose: The 3W-NO. strategy reminds kids of the information to leave on a voice message in order for the message to be understood and responded to.

Strategy Display

Before leaving a voice message, go through the parts of the 3W-NO. strategy in your head. Then tell

- Who is calling
- When you are calling
- What you are calling for

Finally, leave a Number at which you can be reached.

Quick Tips

- Invited sharing of instances when phone messages (received or left) were confusing; elicit reasons as to why this happened.
- Have students practise 3W-NO. with a peer.

Listening

Problem: **Many kids (and adults) do not know how to listen compassionately to their peers' concerns. They fail to respond appropriately, leaving all involved dissatisfied or uncomfortable — a breakdown in communication.**

PUP

Please
Use
Positives

Purpose: PUP is a strategy that teaches a few prime do's and don'ts of affective and effective listening and communicating, with the emphasis being on use of positive responses.

Strategy Display

Sometimes, another person will share a confidence with you. When someone is talking to you about important and perhaps even uncomfortable situations or problems, you need to be very aware of how you respond. Beyond listening carefully, you can reply in certain ways that will be helpful to both of you.

- Respond in ways that show you understand what others are going through, what their concerns are.
- Let them know they have a right to their feelings even if you don't agree.
- Ask questions and listen carefully to the responses.
- Imagine how you'd feel if you were in the situation someone is telling you about. What might help you to better accept or deal with it? What would you like to hear if you had shared the same confidence? With this in mind, provide positive feedback.
- Describe your own feelings rather than evaluating those of others.

Quick Tips

- Using the strategy name, PUP, discuss how to handle a puppy (in a warm, affectionate, accepting manner).
- Discuss how to apply this approach to conversations.
- Practise focusing on appropriate non-verbal cues as these are more convincing than verbal cues. For example, if discussing something sad, be sure not to grin.

Problem: **Too often, students (and people in general) do not listen actively. This aspect of communication, when it is weak, contributes to many mixed messages and consequent frustrations.**

LE-LE

Listening Eyes
Looking Ears

Purpose: The LE-LE strategy (pronounced leelee) reminds kids that listening involves more than just being there. In order to be good listeners, they must pay close attention, look carefully at the speaker, watch for non-verbal cues, and try to determine exactly what the speaker means.

Strategy Display

- Give the speaker your full attention — do not look away, fidget, or daydream.
- Watch the speaker closely, especially the eyes.
- Pay attention to nuances of behavior, for example, restless hands or bouncing knees; try to understand how these affect what is being said.
- Mentally record all non-verbal cues the speaker is giving.

Quick Tips

- Discuss what it feels like to talk to someone who is looking elsewhere. What are the good manners of listening?
- Discuss what it means to listen with your eyes and look with your ears. (Both refer to watching the speaker.)
- Demonstrate: say something to the students several times, using different non-verbal cues each time. For instance, say, "I have so much to do tonight, I may just have to do nothing." First time, look happy, arms wide with palms up, looking like you love this idea. Second time, look upset. Make fists; then, nibble nails. Third time, look confused. Scrunch face, rub forehead, and sigh.
- In pairs, practise first bad, then good, listening techniques.

HEAR

Halt
Evaluate
Ask
Respond

Purpose: The HEAR strategy reminds kids of the most important actions to take when listening to another person. It is particularly useful when the teacher is providing information in a lecture or other traditional format or when directions are being delivered.

Strategy Display

When you need to hear, to really listen, do the following:

   Halt everything else you are doing and focus on the speaker.

Evaluate what is being said by consciously linking the information to what you already know.

Ask questions periodically if or when you are confused or need the speaker to repeat or clarify a point.

Respond to the speaker by summarizing, note-taking, agreeing, or disagreeing. The response is dependent on the speaker's purpose.

Quick Tips

- Discuss the importance of active listening. Perhaps invite kids to share examples of "miscommunication" due to poor listening skills. Share a few of your own examples if they do not disclose.
- Discuss the difference between appearing to listen and really hearing and connect to the HEAR strategy.
- Discuss each step of the HEAR strategy. Practise together by inviting a student to read a passage to the class during which you all actively employ HEAR.

Persuasion

Problem: **Being able to persuade, either in written or oral format, is a necessary life skill not usually perfected by our students.**

P-LEA-SE

Purpose: The P-LEA-SE strategy serves to remind kids of the best way to present an oral or written persuasion; at the same time, it subtly reminds them to be polite while doing so.

Position
List Each Argument
Strong End

Strategy Display

When you need to present an argument or attempt to persuade, use the following steps:

1. Clearly state your Position. This is your stand or "reason" for wanting others to agree with you.
2. List Each Argument or present additional points of support for your position clearly and concisely.
3. Present your Strong End, or most powerful reason or point. Saving the best for last is an effective bargaining ploy.

Keep in mind the importance of maintaining good manners throughout an oral argument.

Quick Tips

- Begin with a discussion of times when kids have had to persuade someone — for example, a parent — to let them do something, such as attend a party, mall, or movie.
- Invite them to share ideas about what worked and what didn't work so well.
- Introduce the P-LEA-SE strategy and practise it together.
- Introduce a fictitious situation and allow kids to develop persuasive arguments in small groups, using the strategy. Sample situations:

You want the school principal to allow Friday assemblies.
You want your parents to let you have a big party.
You want the community council to build a new playground.

Communicating in Writing

Problem: **The entire realm of e-mail communication can be problematic for students. It is far too easy to push "Send Now" and immediately wish that the mail could be retrieved.**

SMART

Send
Mail
After
Rereading
Thoroughly

Purpose: The extremely useful SMART strategy reminds kids not to push "Send Now" on the computer until they are very sure they want that message read not just by the receiver, but possibly by many others as well.

Strategy Display

1. Write the e-mail message.
2. Do not push "Send Now." First, *critically* read what you have written. In other words, carefully look for errors and determine if what you've written is truly what you want to say.
3. Even after rereading your message, wait at least five seconds before sending. Employing a five-second rule will ensure you have reread your message thoroughly. Avoid the temptation to write mail and push all in one movement.
4. Push "Send Now" after you are sure that your message is ready to be transmitted — keep in mind that once sent, the message cannot be retrieved.

Quick Tips

- Discuss instances when e-mail messages have caused problems. (Most kids will be able to relate to this. If not, share a personal experience. I *know* you've had more than one.)
- Discuss the possibility of the e-mail being read by others than whom it was intended for.
- Discuss the five-second rule and draw from kids its importance.

Problem: **Letter writing, whether via e-mail or snail mail, is an important form of communication at which many kids (as well as many adults) fail to excel.**

MAY-I

Me Answer You–
Interrogate

Purpose: The MAY-I strategy reminds us of the most important content of a good letter, either formal or informal. By applying this strategy, kids will know they have included the most important details.

Strategy Display

Me: Begin by saying who you are (formal) or telling something interesting about yourself.

Answer: Respond to any questions the receiver may have asked previously or to questions you think they might want answers to.

You: Include information about the other person. Comment on what you know about them or their business (formal) or comment on personal activities or attributes of the receiver, as in "Grandma, I hear you just got a new wide-screen TV — I can hardly wait to see it."

Interrogate: Ask questions you would like to have answered in a return correspondence.

Quick Tips

There will be complete lessons about letter form during initial instruction phases. The MAY-I strategy is shared after kids know the basics of letter writing, as a reminder about content only.

- Discuss the familiar game May I? Draw connections between it and the MAY-I strategy. (Both are communication; both involve questions and answers and at least two people.)
- Discuss the importance of letters, either formal or informal — whichever you are teaching according to curriculum mandates.
- You may wish to share on overhead a sample of a poor letter (one that talks only about the writer and says nothing about the receiver) and a good one. The key is to get kids to realize the importance of thinking about others in any form of communication.

Problem: **Writing narrative or exposition is one of the most powerful forms of communication — and many of our students struggle terribly with it. They can't seem to get their thoughts on paper and have particular problems when it comes to getting started.**

BAD

Brainstorm
All
Directions

Purpose: The BAD strategy — which, incidentally, kids love to use because of the name "BAD" — serves as a reminder to do lots of rehearsal before beginning to write.

Strategy Display

1. Talk about the topic, or if alone, talk to yourself out loud about the topic. Brainstorm in All Directions — say whatever comes to mind.
2. Play Word Association. Say a word related to the topic and then say the next word that comes to mind, and just keep going.

   Topic: Pets
   Related words: dogs, fun, leash, feed, walk . . .

   Jot down the words as you say them anywhere on a page. Don't worry about organization. Write all over. Be really *bad* with organization.
3. Go back and circle the better words, ones you think you could include in your writing.
4. Rewrite these words on a different page and then choose the best one to include in your first sentence.

Quick Tips

- Rehearsal, or pre-writing, is perhaps the most important and most overlooked part of the writing process. By teaching and reminding kids to use the BAD strategy, we are reinforcing the importance of this stage.

- Demonstrate how to brainstorm in all directions by modelling word or thought association.
- Encourage filling an entire page with divergent ideas or words. These don't all have to be in context; they are just random thoughts. This is the BAD strategy.
- As soon as you have applied BAD, you might want to go immediately to using one of the organizing strategies, such as Ladder (page 46), RAFTS (pages 43–44), or W-W (page 45).

Problem: **Because writing is a valid form of communication, following the rules of good writing is an example of "courtesy" to the reader; however, many kids fail to edit or review their writing.**

S2-P2-C2

Purpose: The unusually named S2-P2-C2 strategy reminds kids of the six important areas to check when writing for an audience: Sentences, Spelling (vocabulary), Paragraphs (content), Punctuation (conventions), Catchy start (introduction), and Conclusion (organization).

Strategy Display

This strategy is presented as a checklist that students can apply to their writing. See the line master on the next page.

Quick Tips

- Begin by sharing a poorly edited piece of writing (yours — not a student's) and discuss the idea of "being impolite to the reader" by not taking care with the editing.
- Go through the poorly written exemplar together, applying the S2-P2-C2 editing strategy.
- Point out that not all writing needs editing. For example, journals, writing for self as audience, and text messaging do not.

Problem: **Some kids, often referred to as "apathetic writers," balk at any type of writing. Getting these unmotivated and reluctant students to write can be a monumental task.**

MAKE-A-DEAL

Purpose: The Make-a-Deal strategy encourages reluctant writers to write something by appealing to their love of deals and games and allowing them a choice. It also makes them feel in control of the situation.

Strategy Display

1. Explain the assignment to the student and then ask how much of it the student will write. The amount might be one paragraph, half the assignment, one sentence, or just the ending — the key is to keep increasing the agreed-upon portion with each assignment.
2. Barter with the reluctant writer until you feel satisfied that he or she will complete the agreed-upon portion.

Sentences **S**pelling
Paragraphs **P**unctuation
Catchy start **C**onclusion

One student called S2-P2-C2 the "robot" strategy as he felt it sounded like the name of a robot.

There are so many different approaches to getting kids to edit, and all of them are lacking in some way. Perhaps due to the unusual nature of its name, the S2-C2-P2 seems to catch them better than many other strategies I have used.

Although the following two strategies are mainly for teacher use to help students to write, they can be adopted for personal student use by showing students how to "make-a-deal" with themselves or use Quid Pro Quo alone. Suggestions follow each strategy. Unlike other strategies in this book, the Strategy Displays presented here are written strictly for the teacher, not the student.

The S2-P2-C2 Strategy

Use the S2-P2-C2 strategy every time you write and need a finished product. Check off each component as you review it.

Sentences

- Do my sentences have varied beginnings and lengths?
- Are all sentences correctly composed with complete subjects and predicates?
- Have I avoided run-on sentences and sentence fragments?

Spelling

- Is my spelling correct?
- Have I used a thesaurus for "better" words, spelled correctly?

Paragraphs

- Is each paragraph indented?
- Is there one main idea per paragraph?
- Does each paragraph flow into the next?
- Is there interesting information in each paragraph?
- Does each paragraph stick to the point?

Punctuation

- Does each sentence contain correct punctuation? (For example, direct quotations are set within double quotation marks.)

Catchy start

- Does the beginning hook the reader?
- Does it make sense with what's to come?

Conclusion

- Does the conclusion tie it all up and flow with what's happened?
- Does it relate back to the beginning or, because of its clever content, leave the reader wondering and even wanting more?

Teachers will recognize this as a "shaping" and "scaffolding" procedure.

3. Later, reinforce completion of the agreed-upon component and remind the student that more will be expected next time.

Quick Tips

- Do not try to "force" the student to write more than is bartered for.
- Increase expectations with each task.
- Remember that *any* writing is better than *no* writing, and small successes will lead to greater ones.

Student Individualization

Discuss the Make-a-Deal strategy as a plan of attack individuals can use without teacher intervention. Students can make the deal with themselves and keep increasing the expectations. Explain that adults often use this technique for many activities other than writing. For example, they may make a personal deal to exercise five minutes more each day to a maximum of 30 minutes.

QUID PRO QUO

Quid Pro Quo

Purpose: The Quid Pro Quo strategy encourages the involvement of a reluctant or unmotivated writer by "sharing" the writing task and giving the writer control over what and how much he or she writes.

Strategy Display

1. The teacher offers an initial sentence in the writing.
2. The student adds the second sentence.
3. The teacher adds the third and so on until the composition is completed, both teacher and student choose to stop, or the student chooses to finish independently.

Quick Tips

- Discuss the concept of quid pro quo (something for something) with the student(s).
- Discuss how life is often full of give and take and how the Quid Pro Quo strategy can help them to deal with others, as in sharing chores with siblings.
- Offer to work with a specific student(s) using this strategy, pointing out that this measure will be temporary as opposed to all the time.
- Each time the student adds a sentence, provide specific, positive reinforcement, for example: "I like the way you tied that sentence to my sentence by starting with . . ."

3

Organizing

Trying to do anything in the midst of confusion is impossible. Disorganization is the forerunner of overwhelming feelings of being scattered, muddled, and frustrated. Most certainly these are *not* the upsetting sentiments we want our students to experience. So let us teach them strategies that will help them organize their lives.

When I speak of disorganization, I am not referring to just the *physical* confusion of a messy desk, backpack, locker, or notebook. I am also referring to disorganization of the mind. This latter state may well be the downfall of even the best student if it is not addressed. Internal disorganization leads to stress which, in turn, leads to further disorganization and frustration; hence, the proverbial never-ending circle. By helping our students to deal with "mind disorganization" (for we cannot ever completely remove it), we are giving them important life strategies.

Reams have been written about how to get organized. For the purpose of this book, however, I will present only specific, simple strategies that students can directly use and see immediate positive results. These strategies address problems common to kids of all ages and to most adults as well. Perhaps you'll find a couple of useful ones yourself.

If we could all be calm, organized adults who lead purposeful and structured lives, wouldn't life be beautiful? Impossible, I know, but surely a lofty ideal. It is possible to lean towards that model; the strategies in this chapter will help kids in that respect. Consider the engulfing calm within a Zen-type garden. This may represent the definitive organization; every line in the sand as well as every stone on the grass is precise and calculated. Drawing students' attention to this intriguing type of garden may be an excellent introduction to any strategy about organization. Ultimately, the purpose of this chapter is to provide ways for teachers to help students (and perhaps themselves) to achieve a measure of calm in their lives, something that cannot be reached if they are surrounded by chaos.

Areas addressed in this chapter include

- separation of essential from nonessential details in reading and listening
- accumulation of material "stuff"
- sequencing of material for learning
- writing practices that allow for planning and editing
- organization for getting started in writing
- mind "clutter" and how to deal with the accompanying anxiety
- graphic organizers
- time organizers

Clearing Out

Problem: **An accumulation of "junk" prohibits the finding and using of what is important.**

TOSS

Throw
Out
Superfluous
Stuff

For younger students, substitute "Silly" for "Superfluous."

Purpose: The TOSS strategy encourages kids to regularly toss or throw out unwanted or unused superfluous stuff.

Strategy Display

Weekly Toss: Once a week, apply TOSS to desks and backpacks. Remove all unnecessary "stuff" and trash it.

Biweekly Toss: Apply TOSS to notebooks. Throw out loose pages (but read them first), scribble pages, or pages you no longer need. If unsure, remove pages from binders and "store" extra pages in a bin or box, rather than throwing them out.

Monthly Toss: Apply to personal spaces, such as closets and bedrooms. If you haven't worn an article for six months, consider giving it away, discarding it, or at least storing it elsewhere to help get rid of closet clutter. Once this has been done, complete a Monthly Toss worksheet and hand it in.

Quick Tips

- Discuss the importance of lack of clutter for efficient work, study, and general living. It has been proven that clutter is not conducive to healthy living, learning, or inner calm.
- Together, do a toss with some space in the classroom, perhaps a drawer or cupboard.
- Encourage kids to use the TOSS strategy whenever they feel "cluttered."
- You may wish to discuss how TOSS can work with minds, too. It can be a cleansing technique whereby students consciously try to empty unnecessary "stuff" from their minds before, for example, a test or study situation. They can do this by deep breathing and visualizing a black slate or empty room. (See page 12.)

Organized Ordering

Problem: **Often, kids work hard at learning and remembering, only to "forget" much of what they think they have mastered. The cause is often the lack of organization or sequence of presented or studied material.**

REORDER

Reorder

Purpose: Research indicates that what is learned first and last (at the beginning and ends of a session) is most recalled. The Reorder strategy teaches kids how to change their study style to build on this knowledge.

Strategy Display

1. Look at a chunk of material to be learned and remove by highlighting, underlining, or in some other way the most important parts.

Monthly Toss

Items tossed: _____

_____

_____

Tell where each item was tossed *from* or where it was tossed *to*.

Examples:

The broken tennis racquet was removed from my bedroom closet.
The red jacket that is too small for me was given to a younger cousin.

1. _____

2. _____

3. _____

Briefly explain how you felt about the toss. You can write about this generally or consider how you felt about tossing certain items.

Examples:

It felt good to have a tidy desk.
I sort of hated to part with my old play easel, but after it was gone I really didn't miss it.

_____

_____

_____

_____

_____

_____

2. Study or learn these at the beginning of the session; then, review at the end of the session.
3. Use the middle time for looking at less important details.
4. Repeat this procedure with all chunks, or pages, paragraphs, sections, and chapters under consideration.

Quick Tips

- Discuss how to determine the most important parts of a text, article, or presentation. Suggest examination of the following:

  key words, boldfaced headings and subheadings, illustrations, graphics, diagrams, or charts, changes in font size, sequences, lists, text bullets

- Invite kids to read, study, or pay attention to these areas first and last.

Problem: **Too often, the cliché "can't see the forest for the trees" describes what happens when students try to organize information for memory. They get swamped by the myriad details and become lost or, at the very least, bogged down. Although this may at first seem like a "memory" problem, it falls under the organization umbrella as it is initially an organizational task.**

UMBRELLA

Purpose: The Umbrella strategy reminds students to organize by first considering or getting the "big picture," then attaching the details to it.

Strategy Display

1. Quickly scan the entire section to be learned.
2. Examine headings, boldfaced print, charts, and such before reading the details.
3. Draw out the general or main idea(s), as in North America has many valuable resources.
4. Visualize these as an umbrella, under which all the smaller ideas and details will fit. See Figure 1.

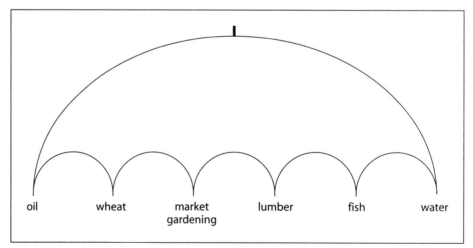

Figure 1. Umbrella strategy applied to topic of North American resources

5. Look at or read details and as you do, place them under the umbrella mentally or by jotting them down on paper (e.g., oil, wheat, lumber, water).

Quick Tips

- Discuss the concept of an umbrella as a main idea covering all smaller ideas.
- Draw an umbrella on the board; label it with a topic or theme.
- Together, place many details under the umbrella. The visual aspect of this promotes the understanding of the "big picture."

FIT

File
It
Topically

This may seem an impossible task, but if you make an effort to categorize incoming information in order to FIT it, there is a much greater chance of it being remembered. The organization of received data prompts memory.

Purpose: The FIT (pronounced "fit") strategy encourages kids to keep their brains in shape, or fit, by organizing information as it is received.

Strategy Display

1. When information is being received through any modality (listening, viewing, reading), make a point of deciding where in your brain to store it. If, for example, the information is related to math, consciously store it with other math-related concepts.
2. When you have completed the receiving aspect, recheck to see if you mentally filed it in the correct place or if some of the information may need to be filed elsewhere.

Quick Tips

- Discuss the concept of being physically fit and draw the connection to being mentally fit.
- Discuss how we put things in specific files, either manually or on the computer, and draw the connection to mentally filing information the same way.
- Do a few examples together. Suggestions: In what mental file would I put information about

    the density of an element
    the formula for circumference of a circle
    the creation of a good sentence

Problem: When kids are faced with a writing project, they can feel daunted. Perhaps their ideas are in freefall and they can't get started, or their thoughts are too random, too "large" and unfocused to make writing possible. Getting organized to begin is the problem here.

RAFTS

Role
Audience
Form
Topic
Strong word

Purpose: RAFTS is a great get-going strategy for kids of all ages and abilities, quickly taking them from a blank page to a beginning writing. A valuable rehearsal strategy, it never fails to help overcome the "Teacher,-I-don't-know-what-to-write" syndrome.

Strategy Display

Write the letters *R, A, F, T,* and *S* vertically on a page or board. Beside each letter, write one or two words of explanation, similar to those below. Brainstorm ideas for topic(s) and strong word(s). (Other letters will be predetermined by situation, teacher, or student.)

R (Role): From whose point of view will the writing come? Examples: First person (I and me), second person (you), third person (he/she), or animal or inanimate object (tree)

A (Audience): For whom is the piece being written? Is the audience general, as in anybody/everybody will be able to read it? (This audience is the most common.) Is it personal? Is it for the teacher? older or younger children? parents?

F (Form): What structure will the writing take? Examples: Essay, paragraph, letter, narrative

T (Topic): What will the writing be about? Here, a general topic, such as pets, is usually made more specific (e.g., caring for pets). Kids narrow the topic to a manageable chunk.

S (Strong word): What strong word, likely a verb, will appear in the first sentence to hook, or interest, readers to continue? Or, as an alternative, what strong word represents the overall *purpose* of your writing? Is the purpose to persuade? enlighten? entertain? amuse? educate? encourage?

Quick Tips

- Discuss how a raft can save your life if you are stuck in the water. Compare this to the metaphorical saving done by RAFTS as a pre-writing strategy.
- Set guidelines for whatever components you wish to control. For instance, if you want kids to write an essay, tell them that the *F*, in this case, signifies essay. Similarly, if you want to give a broad topic, help them to focus or specify an area within the topic *before* they begin writing. You can do this by using a visual cue, such as represented by the Umbrella strategy (pages 42–43) and having students write about a detail under the "umbrella theme." You can also do this by discussing, as a class, the many aspects of the topic; then, in small groups or with partners, students identify specific components of the topic and select favorites about which to write. In most cases, these "specific components" will be approved by you, as a final check for viability, before the writing begins. Usually, teachers control *A, F,* and *T* (to some degree), but these can all be left to the students, providing them with many choices.
- Go through the RAFTS strategy as a class first. Provide a topic of general interest and use the chalkboard or overhead to complete one or two different RAFTS based on that topic.
- Point out that RAFTS is merely a temporary measure, just as someone makes only temporary use of a life raft; what is written can be changed once the writing begins.

Completing more than one RAFTS outline serves not only as a modelling activity, but also shows students how a single topic can be approached in varying ways.

W-W

Purpose: The W-W strategy is a slight deviation from the familiar "web" with which most kids are all too familiar. It encourages quick, almost random jotting of ideas on a page and connecting them afterwards with color or shape. The Wild Web strategy seems to be easier for kids to use than the traditional mind web. Although similar to the BAD strategy (Communicating), there is more organization to it.

Strategy Display

1. Brainstorm the topic and write words, ideas, and phrases all over a blank page.
2. Using either different colored pencils or shapes, group similar ideas together.
3. Draw lines connecting similar groups (see Figure 2).

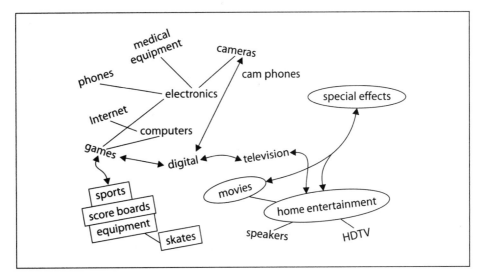

Figure 2. Wild Web on the theme of technology

4. Number groups according to importance.
5. Closely examine uncolored or unmarked words; if these are now deemed unnecessary or repetitious, cross them out.
6. The grouped words/ideas go together to make individual paragraphs.

Quick Tips

- Do a Wild Web together. The bigger, the more detailed, the "wilder," the better. Use an entire board if possible.
- Encourage brainstorming with peers before students create individual Wild Webs.
- Remind kids that on these Wild Webs, spelling, grammar, and neatness are not important.

Ladder

The idea of a pyramid works equally well for this strategy. I have adopted the Ladder image because some students liked the idea that the higher they got on the ladder, the better their organizing got.

LADDER

Purpose: The Ladder strategy provides a visual skeleton that incorporates gradual reduction of ideas from general to specific.

Strategy Display

1. Use a copy of a Ladder provided by the teacher, or draw your own by first making two slightly converging lines, wide at the bottom of the page, narrower at the top. You can add the "rungs" (horizontal lines) as needed. Some rungs will be farther apart than others. (See Figure 3.)

2. Following rehearsal discussion of the topic, fill in the lowest space with as many words, thoughts, and ideas related to your chosen topic as you can. The example in Figure 3 is based on the topic of holiday.

3. In the next space up, which will be slightly smaller, write the more important of the words from the bottom space. You may have to combine some ideas into a more concise form — you are beginning to "narrow" the broad focus of your initial topic or theme by making conscious selections.

4. In the third space from the bottom, again select the words that suggest the specifics about which you will write. By now you will have an idea about just how you will approach the topic. Choose words that are related in some way. In Figure 3, for example, the words relate to camping.

5. Continue reducing the ideas until you reach the top rung (space) on the Ladder. By now the original concept will have been shortened into a workable construct from which you can plan your writing. Using Figure 3 ideas, you may end up with just "pack appropriately" on the top rung. Now, you can write about packing appropriately to go camping, a great topic encompassed by the huge topic "Holiday."

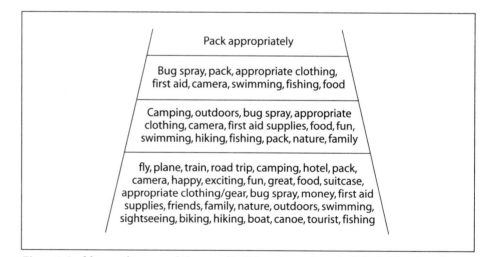

Figure 3. Ladder on the general theme of holiday: As students build a ladder from base to top, they narrow their topic for writing to a manageable size.

Quick Tips

- Discuss how to make a point by finding the most concise way to express something in writing.

- Discuss the importance of narrowing a topic into a manageable chunk for writing. Invite students to share experiences they may have had when a topic was unmanageable or out of control.
- Discuss use of thesaurus to find "better" or different words that will help to clarify their writing once they have narrowed the topic.
- Together, use a Ladder to go from a general topic to a more specific one.

D-A-U DOUBLEQ

Description
Action
Unbelievable
Question
Quotation

Here is a mnemonic to help remember the strategy name:

Don't Always Underestimate Quiet Queens.

Purpose: The D-A-U doubleQ strategy reminds kids of the best ways to begin a narrative: it prevents beginning with a boring "Once-upon-a-time" sentence.

Strategy Display

1. Think of the beginning of your story. What do you want to tell the reader immediately? Is it about the protagonist? the setting? the problem?
2. Decide exactly how this will tie into the rest of your story. How will the first paragraph lead to the next sentence or paragraph?
3. Then, choose one of the following types of story starters as the basis for your first sentence and draft it.

   - *Description* — vivid and colorful
   - *Action* sequence
   - *Unbelievable* or compelling statement — a massive exaggeration or a fantastical idea
   - *Question*
   - *Quotation* — interesting, catchy dialogue

Quick Tips

- Discuss good story starters by sharing some with kids. Read the "catchy" opening sentences from a few stories or books and invite students to explain how these sentences "hook" them. Here are a few examples:

Story Starters

Marvin hated his new sweater; it made him look like a stop sign.

— Description from *Boys Don't Knit* by Janice Schoop

I went to sleep with gum in my mouth and now there's gum in my hair and when I got out of bed this morning I tripped on the skateboard and by mistake I dropped my sweater in the sink while the water was running and I could tell it was going to be a terrible, horrible, no good, very bad day."

— Action sequence from *Alexander and the Terrible, Horrible, No Good, Very Bad Day* by Judith Viorst

I don't know how it happened, but I was the only one who could do it, and it was turning out to be worse than I thought it would be.

— Compelling (unbelievable) statement from *All Is Calm* by Ann Walsh

"Where's Papa going with that ax?" said Fern to her mother as they were setting the table for breakfast."

— Quotation/question from *Charlotte's Web* by E. B. White

- Discuss the D-A-U doubleQ strategy, using the mnemonic "Don't Always Underestimate Quiet Queens" to help recall the letters. Connect the letters to the corresponding "starter" words and discuss.
- Provide practice using each of the different starters in initial paragraphs; then, invite kids to choose and use their favorite to complete a story.
- Note that there are many other colorful ways to begin stories, but the ones presented here are those that students seem to grasp most easily.

Problem: **Some kids cannot organize their writing in such a way that they edit. Once written, the piece is considered finished and the idea of returning to it to make changes is seemingly impossible for them. Often, they write too much too quickly, forfeiting accuracy of conventions and clarity of expression.**

B-B

Building
Blocks

This strategy is a metaphor for writing as building or piling blocks on top of each other. Kids text the name as "B-B," but refer to it as the "Building Blocks" strategy in conversation.

Purpose: The B-B strategy encourages kids to think of each paragraph they write as a building block or brick and to be sure that it is perfect — firm, secure, supportive — before placing another block on top.

Strategy Display

1. Write a paragraph — the first block.
2. Review the paragraph to make sure it says what you want it to say. Don't worry about perfect writing (grammar, spelling, punctuation) yet. Instead, consider the content of the paragraph. Is it clear? Does it make sense? Is it a good paragraph with a single coherent thought or idea? This paragraph should serve as the basis for the rest of the paragraphs.
3. Write the next paragraph and repeat the review-for-content procedure. Does this paragraph flow smoothly from the preceding one? Think of the cement that adheres building blocks to make them fit smoothly together. Your paragraphs must fit smoothly together, but each paragraph must also be strong on its own.
4. Carry on until you reach the final paragraph of your piece of writing.

Quick Tips

- Discuss a building block or a brick. Draw attention to the importance of its solidity or strength. If it is not solid or has an imperfection, then it may crumble with the weight of blocks added on top, and all may fall.
- Make the comparison to writing. Each paragraph is a block that must hold up the rest of the composition. (Once kids grasp the metaphor, they love this strategy.) Discuss what makes a single paragraph strong: properly composed sentences all related to a single point or thought. Each paragraph has its own beginning, middle, and ending.
- Together, write a "solid" paragraph and draw a rectangular block around it to add visual clarity to the idea.
- Check the content of the paragraph. Continue only when the block is strong, when the paragraph fits with the previous one and supports a single thought. You may wish to discuss transition words, such as these:

  then, next, so, although, following

- Write a few more paragraphs together, following the same procedure. End with a "tower" of blocks: a composition that is sound in content and organization, ready for editing.

Using Graphic Organizers

Problem: **Often, reading material is filled with opposing or fluctuating positions, which can make it difficult for students to grasp what is being said. They may experience confusion rather than clarity. This phenomenon can occur, for example, in narratives where a character exhibits a variety of contrary traits or struggles with diverging emotions.**

YIN-YANG

Purpose: The Yin-Yang strategy makes use of the familiar yin-yang symbol and makes the assumption that students are at least minimally aware of how it works. Students are encouraged to see the opposing positions or situations as being interdependent, rather than as being completely divergent, and to place the information accordingly within a yin-yang illustration. (See Figure 4.)

Strategy Display

1. Separate information — facts, character traits, actions, principles in nature — into two major categories. These categories will vary depending upon what is being reviewed. Possible examples are summer and winter, anger and calm, agreement and disagreement.
2. Write the words or concepts in each side of the illustration.
3. Name each side by labeling the small circle within each yin or yang.
4. Examine the complete circle with a view to figuring out how each side affects the other. Look for the interdependence between the two halves and write this as a single statement below the figure.

The yin-yang symbol is a Chinese representation of *everything*: the interior black (yin) and white (yang) represent the interaction of two energies, or, for our purposes, opposites. Neither opposite can exist without the other. The intertwined shape of two colors gives the impression of continual movement — the interdependence of the opposites. All opposites in life — for example, sickness and health — or in fiction, as in the unexpected behavior of a character, can be explained by suggesting that there is a temporary dominance of one principle (yin or yang) over the other.

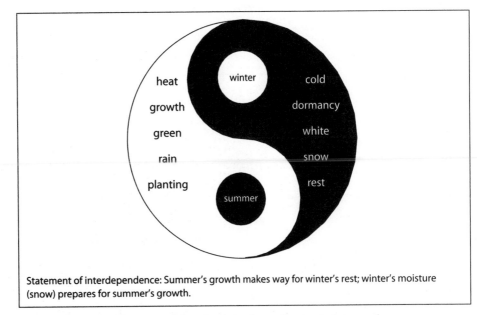

Statement of interdependence: Summer's growth makes way for winter's rest; winter's moisture (snow) prepares for summer's growth.

Figure 4. Yin-yang illustration showing interdependence of winter and summer

Quick Tips

- Discuss the yin-yang drawing.
- Discuss how the specific material can be sorted into two "opposing" categories, keeping in mind that nothing is ever truly black or white.
- Discuss the idea of interdependence as related to the concepts being studied or read about. Use the idea of constant movement or change.
- Invite kids to list the attributes appropriately in the white and black halves. The visual representation of the material will make a lasting impression and clarify organization.

VENN DIAGRAM

Venn diagram

Purpose: The familiar and popular Venn diagram provides a visual comparison between variables or characters.

Strategy Display

1. Draw two large overlapping circles (see Figure 5).

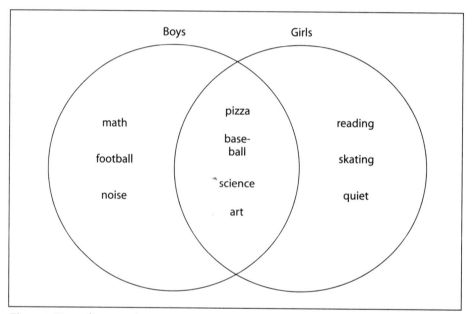

Figure 5. Venn diagram showing generalizations on what boys and girls like

You can use three intersecting circles for a more complex Venn. In this case, the very centre would list traits common to all three variables.

2. Label each circle according to the variable to be compared.
3. In each separate portion of the circles, list the characteristics of that particular variable.
4. In the intersecting portion, list the characteristics common to both.

Quick Tips

- Discuss how variables can have both similar and opposing traits. A Venn is often used with character comparison; a good introductory tactic is to use a Venn to compare self and a story protagonist.
- Suggest neat, horizontal printing within the circle components.
- With younger children, illustrations can be used together with print.
- Point out the importance of naming the circles.
- Create a class Venn, perhaps comparing boys and girls.

SHADOW CHART

Purpose: A Shadow chart is an appealing visual strategy for close examination of a real or fictional character.

Strategy Display

Shadow chart

This strategy is much like the Role on the Wall strategy.

Reassure students that they do not need to worry about how well they draw. The point is that they sketch out a large-enough shadow for writing.

1. Draw a shadow-type outline, perhaps a gingerbread man, to illustrate the character being examined. (See Figure 6.)

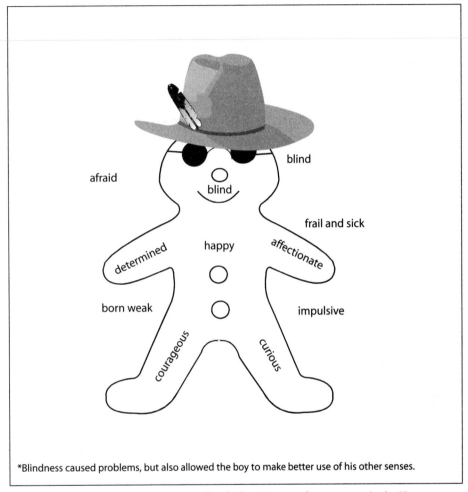

afraid

blind

blind

frail and sick

determined   happy   affectionate

born weak   impulsive

courageous   curious

*Blindness caused problems, but also allowed the boy to make better use of his other senses.

Figure 6. Shadow chart of Boy-Strength-of-Blue-Horses, the protagonist in *Knots on a Counting Rope*, written by Bill Martin Jr. and John Archambault, and illustrated by Ted Rand: The character is a First Nations boy who dresses and rides like a cowboy.

If a certain article of clothing or item, such as a cowboy hat, readily communicates something about a character, you may want to indicate that when making an outline of the shadow figure. Be sure to keep the shadow large and clear.

2. Inside the shadow, write or illustrate all the character's positive characteristics.
3. Outside the shadow, in the negative space around it, indicate all the negative characteristics.

Quick Tips

- It is a good idea to provide a photocopied shadow for younger kids. Once they have the general idea, older students love to create their own shadows, specific to the characters being studied.

- Encourage use of a thesaurus to come up with good describing words and phrases.
- Once the Shadow charts are completed, encourage students to use the descriptions in a writing project.
- Consider displaying the Shadow charts.

TUG OF WAR

Tug of War

Kids love this innovative and visual strategy.

Purpose: The Tug of War strategy is a visual representation of opposing forces or opposites of any nature. It visually depicts where the balance lies (or doesn't lie).

Strategy Display

1. Draw a horizontal line across the middle of the page.
2. Indicate the middle of the line with a heavy, short vertical line.
3. Add a plus sign above one end of the line and a minus sign above the other. At opposite ends of the line, list opposing traits: positives versus negatives, pros versus cons (see Figure 7).

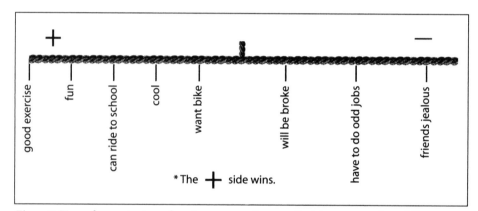

Figure 7. Tug of War strategy showing pros and cons of raising money for a bike

4. When you have listed as many as possible on each end, decide which end wins. In other words, which side has most notes on it? That side would win a tug of war.
5. Write about why you think the result turned out the way it was displayed.

Quick Tips

- Discuss what a tug of war is and how it allows opposing units to face off and ultimately declare a winner based on, in this case, strength.
- Apply this understanding to the Tug of War strategy and demonstrate by doing an in-class comparison of any two variables. Be sure that there are more criteria on one end than on the other.

Making Effective Use of Time

Problem: **Time organization can be one of the most daunting issues for students, especially when so many of them are involved in so many areas other than school.**

Kids love this strategy and will use it readily. I use it daily and find I end up with many minutes for "me" time.

BIAS

Purpose: The BIAS, or Book It And Steal, strategy prompts kids to organize their days to the best of their abilities, using a simple, visual plan, and to "steal" times for fun things by doing so.

Strategy Display

1. Think of the day or part of the day (the part where you choose how to spend your time) as a series of horizontal blocks.
2. Create (draw, use a computer, make a checklist, or otherwise do whatever works for you) a visual that defines periods of time as brief as 10 minutes. (See Figure 8.)
3. Book previously established specific activities such as school, lessons, and practices within the blocks.
4. Look at the empty time blocks and book the duties of that specific day (e.g., homework, studying, and reading). Make good guesses about how many minutes you will need for various tasks. Prepare yourself to see that all your time is accounted for, that no "me" time seems open.
5. The "stealing of minutes" now comes into play. Work with focus and energy to complete the tasks you have had to book in less than their allotted times. The leftover minutes are accumulated and considered "stolen" time just for you.
6. If you were earlier able to allot specific "me" time on your daily agenda, add the stolen minutes to it — that's more time for you to do what you want to do.

6:30–7:00	Math homework	10 min. stolen
7:00–7:15	Read L.A. story	
7:15–7:45	Work on science report	
7:45–8:00	Review spelling	7 min. stolen
8:00–9:00	FREE TIME WITH 17 min. stolen = 7:43–9:00	

Figure 8. BIAS strategy showing a 2.5 hour block of time

Some days you may have more stolen minutes than others and you may be able to carry those minutes on till the next day. For example, if you are working on a project for school and get more done on one day than you expected to, the next day you will have stolen minutes.

7. Be firm with yourself. Don't set any other goal for any particular block. Do not do a task poorly just to save minutes. The goal is to work hard and well and still have time to do things you enjoy.

8. Keep a record of your commitment, perhaps putting an * on the calendar for each day you meet your "me" time page expectations. Pay attention to how well you use allocated time and how often you can steal minutes wisely.

Quick Tips

- Discuss time management problems and point out how important it is for kids to simply set the habit of routine.
- Discuss how we are *biased* when it comes to giving time to things we enjoy doing. Students will tend to allow more time for watching TV than for homework. Connect this idea to the strategy name. Point out how the BIAS strategy helps to avoid this sort of dilemma and to make productive use of time.
- Discuss the importance of personal, or "me," time. (Busy kids often forget this; the results are not positive.)
- Help students create chart-like structures on which to record, or book, their activities and remind them to list lessons and team sports. Kids need to see that these are key time users in their lives and must be accounted for. Encourage them to keep the time blocks within their outlines as brief as possible, ideally 10 to 30 minutes. If an activity requires more time than that, they should consider it as two or three entries, each with a different goal.
- Invite kids to draw their time-block outlines in a way that appeals to them and to print their allotted times and goals neatly within. This visualization assists with establishment of the routine.
- At the end of a week, review with kids how well they were able to apply the strategy. Discuss how and when they were able to steal time for themselves.

4

Discovering

Discovering, for the purpose of this book, refers to finding out about life, uncovering what is needed for successful living, and "locating" the best possible sources of information and assistance for continued personal growth. It is the act of personal construction of meaning as a result of experimentation, questioning, and making of generalizations and inferences. Thus discovering is "different" for everyone. It represents individualized instruction in its truest form, facilitated through use of strategies.

As educators, we are fully aware of the importance of encouraging our students to inquire, to critique, to ask "why?" We appreciate that we cannot teach them everything; the best we can do is give them the tools to find out what they need to know and how to access, tabulate, and recall it. This type of learning should not be exclusive to childhood. It is equally important that adults continue to grow through learning, through persistent expansion of personal knowledge bases and repertoires.

It is also true that with discovery learning, students are more likely to remember what they have learned. The *aha* method of learning is an integral part of being alive. In many ways it is similar to creating, the sixth theme of this book. My differentiation between the two is that while creating comes from within, discovering comes more from without. It is a search-and-find approach to learning and to life.

Many instructional design models are based on discovery learning, but these are not included in this book. Rather I have chosen specific, concise "discovery" strategies that directly involve innovation or detection on the parts of the students, strategies that can be taught in isolation and, it is hoped, remembered forever. Not designed to lead to single, predetermined goals, they are meant for active doing and discovering of facts not previously recognized, whether these be facts about students themselves, about daily living, about others, or about curriculum topics.

Discovering is a cognitive as well as a creative approach to life that involves the ongoing development and refinement of hypotheses. It also involves careful examination of situations, innovative problem-solving, and use of reason. It can often be supported by strategy use.

The areas addressed in this chapter include

- expanding vocabulary
- developing awareness of self
- asking good questions
- seeking advice
- discovering hidden or extra meanings in text
- critiquing communication

Expanding Vocabulary

Problem: **Many students don't take the time to look up new words or actively increase their spoken and/or written vocabularies. Unless kids are regularly encouraged to expand their vocabularies, many take the easy route, using a dictionary or thesaurus only as needed.**

DOUBLE-D

Purpose: The Double-D strategy persuades students to "discover" or find out more about life by adding to their vocabularies daily.

Daily Definition

Strategy Display

1. Find a new, usable word that interests you every day.
2. Keep a record of new words.
3. Use the new words in context when writing and speaking.
4. Choose words to illustrate.

Quick Tips

- Talk about the strategy name, Double-D, and how it signifies Daily Definition.
- For the first week, choose a new, interesting word together each day, and record the word and definition.
- Encourage contextual use of the words and if appropriate, include the words on spelling lists.
- You may assign categories for new words. For example, the words must be related to living things or related to shapes.
- Provide time daily for the sharing of daily definitions.

Exploring Facts

Problem: **Although some kids are "turned on" by the discovery of new facts and information, many simply can't be bothered.**

NOVUS

Purpose: The Novus strategy encourages kids to discover new ideas or facts daily, to keep a record of them, and maybe share them.

Novus

Strategy Display

1. Pick a time when you can plan for a daily five-minute discovery of something completely new.
2. In that discovery time, either locate a new fact in a book, on the Internet, from a friend or adult, or from television.
3. Briefly record the new fact you have discovered in a Novus scribbler.

Quick Tips

- Discuss the meaning of Novus (Latin for new).

- Discuss the importance of constantly "exercising" our brains by discovering new information.
- Share some interesting new fact you have recently discovered. For example:

  > NASA's Phoenix Mars Lander has stuck a fork in Martian dirt for the first time.
  > —FOXNEWS.COMHOME>SCITECH

- Point out that the "discovered" fact(s) need not be complicated or even lengthy; it is the idea of discovering something new that is important.

Problem: **Kids are expected to use the Internet for discovery — for researching topics and quickly finding information — but often they are overwhelmed by data overload.**

NERD

Purpose: The NERD strategy is a comical reminder of how to effectively and quickly make use of the Internet.

Strategy Display

Narrow
Engine
Review
Date

1. **N**arrow the topic by identifying key words.
2. Use a search **E**ngine by entering the key words.
3. **R**eview the number of choices provided by the engine. If too many are offered, reduce the number of key words entered.
4. **D**ate and reference any information recorded.

Quick Tips

- Draw attention to the meaning of the word "nerd" and how it is often connected to users of computers. Kids love the idea of consciously being nerds.
- Obviously, there is a great deal more to using the Internet than the NERD strategy suggests. Point out that this is a getting-started strategy only.
- Teach lessons about note taking and data gathering together with the NERD strategy.

Self-Discovery

Problem: **Seeking answers to personal-interest questions is not something most kids do automatically. They may have many queries about themselves, but generally no steps are taken to find answers. This process of self-discovery is lacking.**

P-QUEST

Personal
QUESTionnaire

It is "P"-Quest because the questions being researched originate directly from a personal query or interest.

Purpose: P-Quest encourages kids to come up with one or more questions based on a personal query or interest and then prepare and administer a questionnaire in order to formulate a meaningful generalization.

Strategy Display

1. Design a question for which you want an answer. Possibilities: (1) What is the favorite junk food of Grade 3 students? (2) Is your family doing its part to help with waste management?
2. Design a personal questionnaire that includes one or more questions that directly address your initial query. Examples: (1) What three junk foods do you eat most often? Which is your favorite? Why? (2) Does your family use a green bin for organics and limit trash to three bags every two weeks? Do you help pick up the trash in community areas, such as parks, walkways, and around the rink?
3. Obtain responses to your personal questionnaire from a cross-section of people.
4. Find a way to determine the response patterns of the people surveyed. For example, count up each of the favorite junk foods of Grade 3 students to see the order in which foods were identified.
5. Prepare a generalization. Generalizations can be written or preserved in whatever manner is feasible, perhaps through illustrations, cartoons, posters, or drama skits.

Quick Tips

- Point out that P-Quest stands for "Personal QUESTionnaire," but is also a *quest*. Discuss the meaning of the word "quest." Discuss what makes this quest "personal" — that the questions are theirs alone.
- Discuss questions or concerns the kids might have and assess whether these could easily be addressed by a questionnaire.
- Based on a class concern, write a questionnaire together, and invite kids to return the next day with at least 5 to 10 responses. (Hint: Limit the questions to between two and five.)
- Collate questionnaire responses the following school day and make a class generalization.
- Brainstorm how the P-Quest strategy can be useful to them. The following true example exemplifies this and illustrates how the strategy helped a Grade 4 student to "discover."

Discovery Through P-Quest

"Teacher, I sure got a surprise. I did a P-Quest. I wanted to know how everyone felt about rap music. I thought I already knew, but I did a P-Quest anyway and boy, was I wrong! My gram answered that she LIKED rap music because it was FUNKY and she admired the way they could make all the lines rhyme without figuring them out ahead of time. Go figure, hey? I could have sworn that old people hated rap music. So in the end, more than 75 percent of the people I surveyed LIKED rap music. Guess I need a bigger survey, but I sure found out something about old people that I didn't know before! That P-Quest thing is cool!"

Next Life

This strategy is useful at any time when kids feel distressed about their lots in life.

NEXT LIFE

Purpose: The Next Life strategy invites kids to take a good look at themselves — at who they are as opposed to who they'd like to be — and to determine what they can change and what they cannot change at any given moment. It invites realistic interpretation of personal lives.

Strategy Display

1. Determine exactly what you find worrisome at the moment.
   You failed a test.
   You can't afford to go to the movies.
2. Close your eyes and imagine who you'd like to be in your next life. This person can be real or imaginary. Examples:
   a genius like Albert Einstein
   Donald Trump's offspring
3. Think of one positive and one negative about being in that selected Next Life.
   (Positive) I wouldn't have to study as much; (Negative) I would be expected to spend all my time solving the world's problems.
   (Positive) I could afford anything I wanted; (Negative) My privacy would be gone completely.
4. Evaluate the negative as opposed to the positive.
5. Brainstorm ways that you, in your present life, can be more like that Next Life person right now.
   I can plan study time more efficiently.
   I can save allowance or do extra chores.

Quick Tips

- Discuss the idea of wishing to be someone else.
- Connect this to potential problems associated with this other person's existence. (Kids often find this to be a wake-up call because they tend to believe only they have problems.)
- Point out that we can take one specific aspect from the lives of our Next Life characters, and add them to our present lives, to see positive improvements. In the students' choices of Next Life characters lie specific reasons for the choices. It is these reasons we want them to identify and act upon where possible. If the reasons are related to something they cannot alter (e.g., height or body shape), they can instead alter their reasons for wanting the change. For example, for Next Life, someone wants to be a fashion model, really thin and beautiful; she can't change height, but can work on posture and personal hygiene.

S-D-T

Purpose: The S-D-T strategy involves the representation strand of the English language arts curriculum in a personal pursuit activity.

Strategy Display

1. Begin by finding out as much as possible about your family tree and keeping a record of the information.

2. Ask parents and relatives for information about and photographs of family history.

3. Use a large sheet of paper (at least 11 by 14) and begin recording your found information. Use a collage technique. Be sure to avoid "questioning" what you should or shouldn't add to the tapestry — just keep accumulating.

4. Add to the collage until you cannot add any more. Consider the following on your self-discovery tapestry:

> Things, people, places I like
> Hopes for the future
> Personal skills, hobbies, abilities
> Past experiences that have affected me today (camping trip, visit to . . .)

5. When the tapestry is completed, take the time to analyze it. What have you learned about yourself that you didn't previously know?

Quick Tips

- Discuss the powerful effect of family on everyone.
- Invite kids to begin researching their "pasts" and collecting data. (Do not share the S-D-T strategy until data collection has begun.)
- Share the S-D-T strategy, and provide necessary tapestry materials, such as colored paper, scissors, paper and craft glue, buttons, bits of fabric, ribbon or bias tape, any scrapbooking materials from craft stores, photos, and catalogues (for cutting up). Basically, any odds and ends in the classroom can be added to the tapestries.
- You may wish to talk about tapestries and their origins, or invite students to research in this area. One of many excellent Websites on tapestries is http://www.millefleurstapestries.com/2124.

A Brief History of Tapestries

Tapestries originated in the Middle Ages mainly as a means to insulate medieval rooms from damp and cold. The earliest tapestries usually depicted a few solitary figures, but as their makers became increasingly skilled, tapestries became more intricate and detailed. Due to their enormous size and intricate beauty, they became a sign of wealth and a form of investment. Today, tapestries are appreciated for their beauty as opposed to their heat-retaining properties.

- Point out that although we are referring to the works that students are creating as "tapestries," they are really collages; however, the term *tapestries* is appropriate because like real tapestries, they are rich representations of life — in this case, students' personal lives.
- Allow kids to work on their Self-Discovery Tapestries for at least two weeks before inviting them to analyze their work and do further self-discoveries based on the tapestries.

Questioning for Information

Problem: **When kids don't ask the right questions to get the answers they seek, frustration and tension can be the result and discovery is limited. Knowing how to identify what is needed and then specifically ask for that information is not a built-in skill.**

S-Q

Specific
Questions

Purpose: The S-Q strategy helps students ask questions that do a better job of discovering the answers they need or want.

Strategy Display

1. Think of what you want to "discover."
2. Ask yourself what kind of question you have: *who, what, where, when, why,* or *how.* (Most questions fit one or more of these variables.) This is the identification step of questioning.
3. Draft a question that begins with the variable you identified. Keep the wording as simple, concise, and specific as possible.
4. If you do not get an appropriate response, repeat the first three steps.

Quick Tips

- Discuss questioning techniques with kids.
- Provide an open-ended topic, such as whether kids should have a curfew, and invite students to follow the S-Q strategy steps.
- Together, practise making the questions specific, concise, and simple by removing unnecessary words and, if necessary, changing the focus of the questions to make them more specific. For example, rather than ask "Should kids have a curfew?" try: "At what time, should kids between the ages of 7 and 10 be home on week nights?"

WHAT

What
How
Ask
Tabulate

Purpose: The WHAT strategy reminds kids of the necessary components of asking good discovery questions, not just of the necessity to be specific.

Strategy Display

This strategy includes *what* students want to know, *how* they will get that information, whom they will *ask* for assistance, and how they will *tabulate,* or record and manage that information.

1. Decide what you want to discover. Write a question in such a way that the answer will provide you with accurate information. For example, if you want to know something about the newest exhibit at the museum, compose questions such as these: "What sorts of displays are included?" "How would you describe the exhibit?" "Would you recommend the exhibit for Grade 3 students? Why or why not?"
2. Determine how you will discover the answer. Specifically, consider whether you will ask people for responses or research information somewhere.

3. Think of all the people you might ask for assistance or answers, and write a list of names.
4. Go ahead and seek the answers to your questions in the way you have determined.
5. Tabulate all responses and gathered information by answering your initial question.

***Problem*: It is possible that kids often overlook one of the most important resources for discovery — that of the experience of adults.**

ASK

**Approach
Someone
Knowledgeable**

For instance, if a student is struggling with a particular query, you might say, "How could you use the ASK strategy?"

Purpose: The ASK strategy is exactly what its name implies: a reminder to approach someone knowledgeable when help is needed. This strategy may seem frivolous, but sometimes just putting an acronym-name to a familiar action makes it more doable.

Strategy Display

1. Write your question according to the S-Q strategy (see page 61).
2. Brainstorm for all people who may be knowledgeable in this area, and create a written list.
3. Approach the people you listed, elicit responses, and cross the names off the list.

Quick Tips

- Help students put together a class list of people to contact for knowledge in specific areas, for example, the science teacher for information about pollution or the neighborhood grocer for information on meat sources.
- Encourage students to create their own lists of resource persons, including parents, neighbors, and friends.
- Constantly remind them to use the ASK strategy when they begin a new discovery project or have a question of any sort that cannot readily be answered in class. Remind students, as well, that turning to other references — in some cases, before using the ASK strategy — is also a good idea.

SCRAPE

**State
Collect
Research
Arrange
Prioritize
Evaluate**

Purpose: The SCRAPE strategy encourages kids to *scrape* or discover information from someone knowledgeable, using a prepared interview technique.

Strategy Display

State in writing an area of interest. It will represent an area of discovery for you.
Collect a series of questions specifically related to the statement.
Research the person whom you will interview. Find out as much as possible about the person's background, skills, and interests. Determine why you want to interview this person.
Arrange for a time and place for the interview.
Prioritize your questions so that time with the interviewee can be best used.
Evaluate the responses you receive; add them to your discovered information.

Quick Tips

- Discuss the importance of using the experiences of others in a discovery situation. Use the idea of "scraping" together new ideas,
- Practise good interviewing techniques, such as the following, in class.

> Keep the interview quiet and personal. No one should be able to hear except you and the interviewee.
> Be polite, nonjudgmental, and respectful: accept all the answers given to you, even if you don't agree with them.
> Use good listening skills, such as maintaining eye contact, focusing on the speaker, and taking accurate notes.
> If you don't understand something, ask for clarification: "Could you please explain that further?"
> Thank the interviewee at the end, pointing out how the responses supplied will be helpful to you.

- Model how to evaluate and synthesize information received from an interview.

Raising Questions for Deep Understanding

Problem: **Students often want to know "more" about a book they are reading. This natural act of discovery may be difficult to capitalize on unless a specific strategy is used.**

QTA

Questioning the Author

Purpose: The interesting QtA strategy encourages students to "ask the Author" — in pretense only — questions about what has been written, in an attempt to clarify either narrative or informational material.

Strategy Display

1. Think of what you would like to ask the author if you could, to help you better understand the story or article. Either in an oral discussion with peers or in writing, ask the author anything you want to know about such aspects as the characters, setting, or presented information. You might ask for more details or further facts.
2. As if you are the author, answer your questions in writing. Base your responses on what you have read or what you already know. You may find it helpful to do some rereading.

It's OK to have more questions than answers.

3. If you have questions for the author that you can't find or figure out answers to, discuss with peers and try to come up with logical responses.

Quick Tips

The main purpose of the QtA strategy is to get the kids thinking in depth about the story and the author's reasons for writing it a certain way.

- Discuss how everyone takes something different from a story. (Individual differences are allowed for. All answers/responses are deemed correct as long as they are justified by the writing.
- Invite kids to pretend that the author is right there in the room, and they can ask any questions they want about the story. Encourage them to

think of "good" questions, such as those that demand synthesis or analysis, as opposed to factual recall types of questions.

- Have kids write down some of their questions and attempt to answer them. Encourage creative thought; keep reinforcing that there are no wrong answers.
- Remind them that although this strategy seems to call for asking the author questions, they will not in reality ask the author their questions. They will *be* the author when they respond. The question asking and answer seeking help them to clarify their thoughts and frequently to "find" additional, previously missed information. In the case of narratives, they can even embellish facts based on author style and story substance.

Broadening Sources for Discovery

Problem: **The Internet is such a huge draw for kids today that many of the other possible sources of information — places that lead to discovery — are overlooked.**

P-I-T-N-V-L-M-Q-I

Purpose: This strategy name is also a mnemonic for the list of places kids can look to make discoveries. The first letter of each word is the first letter of each discovery location.

Strategy Display

The following are all super sources for finding information. To do a good job of a report or persuasive piece of writing, students should try to use all or as many of these types of sources as possible.

P Posters, pictures, photographs, paintings
I Internet resources
T Television programs; textbooks
N Newspapers
V Videos, DVDs
L Library resources, including encyclopedias and all varieties of books
M Magazines and journals
Q Questionnaires
I Interviews

Quick Tips

- Ask kids where to go to find information. No doubt they will say the Internet first. Prompt and prod until you get as many other sources as possible *before* introducing the P-I-T-N-V-L-M-Q-I strategy.
- Introduce the strategy with the mnemonic name. If kids don't like the mnemonic name, invite them to think of one on their own. It doesn't matter what technique they use as long as it helps them to recall the long list of letters.
- A good idea is to present a single topic for research, divide the class into groups, and have different groups use the different sources, come together, and compare notes.

Here is a mnemonic to help remember the many-letter strategy name:

People **I**n **T**he **N**ews **V**ery **L**ikely **M**ake **Q**uick **I**nterpretations.

Discovering Truth Through Critiquing

Problem: Kids are faced with so much information that it is often difficult for them to determine what's true and what isn't. The entire area of advertising is a good example. In this case, the presence of inaccurate or biased information, such as that provided by ads featuring overly thin models, can be problematic and frequently confusing.

T-B-N-S-T DOUBLE-G

Testimonial
Bandwagon
Name-calling
Snob-appeal
Transfer
Glittering Generalities

Recall this mnemonic acrostic: The Best Noses Smell The Gooey Goodies.

Purpose: The T-B-N-S-T double-G strategy reminds kids of the most common propaganda devices used in advertising, and sometimes in other texts.

Strategy Display

When viewing or listening to advertising, apply the T-B-N-S-T double-G strategy to see through the faulty image(s) being supplied.
> **Testimonial:** Making an association with a popular athlete or person
> **Bandwagon:** Appealing to our need to be part of a group
> **Name-calling:** Pinning a negative image on something that the advertisers want us to dislike or refuse
> **Snob-appeal:** Attracting the attention of people who want to be part of a special or exclusive group
> **Transfer:** Attempting to make us think that attributes such as attractiveness or wealth can be transmitted to us
> **Glittering Generalities:** Using appealing generalities, such as healthy lifestyle or all natural, to make a product or service look better

Quick Tips

- Discuss the advertising devices.
- Invite kids to find examples of each.
- Once they are familiar with the devices, introduce the T-B-N-S-T double-G strategy with the memory sentence. If kids do not like the sentence, invite them to create their own. They can reorder the letters as necessary.
- Remind them to use the T-B-N-S-T double-G strategy frequently.

SAFE

Stereotypes
Author authenticity
Fact/Fiction
Entertaining/Educating

Purpose: The SAFE strategy is a useful tool for making a quick critique of either narrative or expository writing.

Strategy Display

By asking yourself the following questions related to a reading, you can check the validity of the writing; you will also be critiquing it so that you can respond appropriately.

- Does the writing contain any Stereotypes, or stereotypical comments or illustrations?
- Check the Author authenticity. Is the author qualified to write this piece? (For example, a First Nations author writing about a First Nations topic is "qualified.") Has this author written other pieces with similar content?

- Is the piece presented as Fact or Fiction? If Fact, are the facts true? Are they plausible? Are they correctly researched?
- Is the piece designed to be Entertaining, Educational, or both? Does it do either effectively?

Quick Tips

- Discuss how writing affects us, both intellectually and emotionally.
- Discuss how to tell if authors are adequately qualified to write a certain text. Ask questions such as these:

  "Is the author a member of the (race, age, gender, community, profession, . . .) discussed in the story? How do you know?"

  "If not, does the book explain how the author achieved qualifications?" (Author's page, including education)

- Discuss how to determine whether the author is using facts, fiction, or a combination of both. Ask questions such as these:

  "What points seem to contain factual information and how can we check the facts?" Statement: Johnny lived in Edmonton, a city of almost a million people.

  Identify the "fact" in the sentence and determine that it can be checked on the Internet or by contacting the statistics department of the city.

  "What suggests the story is purely fictional?" (Example: fantasy genre)

  "Are there examples of both fact and fiction and if so, how can we check the facts?"

- Point out how sometimes information we think is valid may, in fact, be a figment of the author's imagination. It therefore might not be safe to use it. Connect this to the SAFE strategy.
- Discuss possible purposes for writing the piece. These include the desire to entertain, to educate, to persuade, or to describe. A question to help determine purpose is, "Is the writing mostly fact or fiction, and how does it make you feel when you read it?" (Examples: excited, anxious, informed)

5

Understanding

Understanding is an abstract and almost indefinable construct referring to the ability to be familiar with, to comprehend, and even to appreciate. When it comes to teaching, the notion of understanding or comprehension takes on an even more expansive meaning: it encompasses all the literacy areas as well as core subject content areas. There is so much we want our students to recognize, realize, be familiar with, and value. It's not surprising that so many of us feel intimidated by the huge responsibility of helping kids to understand.

All teachers are familiar with the students who, for example, can read fluently, but don't seem to understand a word of what they have read. Similarly, all adults are familiar with the kids who appear to be listening, but don't seem to understand a word. This concern is huge, especially when kids today are expected to read reams of material independently, to listen and take accurate notes, to glean in-depth and abstract meaning from visuals, and to grasp the "big pictures" almost entirely on their own.

We want our students to participate actively in their own learning and to have and use all the tools for understanding that are automatic to *most* adults *most* of the time. Consequently, many approaches to aiding comprehension, in particular reading comprehension, have been developed throughout the years, with varying degrees of success. I have experienced the greatest victories when I encouraged kids to use specific strategies to help them understand what they are reading, listening, or viewing. These are the strategies offered in this chapter.

It will quickly be noticed that these strategies are organizational strategies as well, and could therefore be presented earlier in this book. I have chosen to offer them in "understanding" as it is my belief that their ultimate goal is that of comprehension of the written material — comprehension *through* organization.

Perhaps before embarking on presentation of strategies for aiding understanding, it would be wise to examine quickly how to evaluate whether or not understanding has occurred. Naturally, there is the specific-question–specific-answer technique employed by all teachers, but there are also general methods for swiftly appraising understanding. One understands if one is able to

- make an accurate prediction
- provide an accurate explanation
- summarize the relevant aspects
- reproduce the information in own words
- follow directions accurately
- solve problems using the new learning
- retain and use the information accurately

For the purposes of this book, understanding will be reduced to its simplest context: that of being able to obtain and retain information from text and voice.

Although all the strategies here address matters related to reading comprehension, this chapter has been structured in the same way as the others.

Specific areas addressed in this chapter include

- predicting
- summarizing
- identifying key points and details
- tapping into personal background knowledge
- generalizing, analyzing, and synthesizing
- visualizing story components
- recognizing author style and purpose

Identifying Details

Problem: **Students frequently read through an entire passage, but have little idea of what they have read. Frequently, details are overlooked or ignored and there may be confusion as to what information is important and what is not.**

D-R-T-A

Purpose: D-R-T-A involves using predictions to focus attention and help organize and clarify what is being read.

**Directed
Reading
Thinking
Activity**

This well-established strategy has been included in this book because of its considerable value.

This same strategy can be used for listening; it is then called D-L-T-A (Directed Listening Thinking Activity) and the same procedure is followed.

Strategy Display

1. Look at the title of your text and any illustrations and make a prediction as to content.
2. Read a short passage (about a page, depending on level of reading) and then check the prediction.
3. Continue making predictions and checking for correctness.

Quick Tips

- Introduce the strategy by name.
- Have students divide a page vertically and write predictions on one side, then indications as to correctness of the predictions on the opposite side.
- Help students to understand why their predictions were or were not correct. What specific words, phrases, or illustrations affected the predictions?

I-NI

**Important
Not Important**

Purpose: The I-NI strategy reminds kids to separate the important and unimportant details when reading.

Strategy Display

1. Be aware that authors provide information that may not be directly important to the plot or story theme. For example, sometimes a great deal of description can be overlooked without having any effect on following the plot.
2. Divide a page into two sections vertically; write "I" on top of the left column and "NI" at the top of the right column.

3. As you read, pay attention to the details by jotting key words in either of the two columns. Important details are those that have a direct effect on the story.
4. When you have finished reading, review your columns to see if any of the details should be moved from one column to the other.
5. Take note of whether there are more important or not important details in the story. Be prepared to suggest why this might be the case.

Quick Tips

- Discuss "details" in a story.
- Specifically, point out some that are both Important and Not Important. The latter are usually added to keep the story flowing, but may not affect the plot.
- Realize that there will be considerable differentiation among students' answers about what is important and not important. This is great as long as they can justify their opinions. This type of analysis of detail and justification greatly aids comprehension.

Seeking Answers

Problem: **There are many ways to seek answers, to find information, or to satisfy curiosity. Sometimes, students seem bound by the single approach of directly examining the text when other methods would probably be more effective.**

REQUEST

Purpose: The ReQuest strategy, which involves shared, give-and-take questioning between student and teacher, is intended to increase understanding of text. The teacher provides a model for good questioning.

ReQuest

The assumption is that learning to ask and answer good questions leads to better understanding.

This in-depth strategy not only improves comprehension, but teaches questioning and responding skills through modelling.

Strategy Display

1. Read a portion of text either alone or with the teacher.
2. Ask two or more questions about the text; your teacher will answer them with book closed. The number of questions asked will depend on what you need explained further.
3. Now, close your book. Listen to and answer the teacher's questions.
4. Read another portion silently; then, first the student and then the teacher asks questions. This back-and-forth questioning continues until the student can accurately predict the end or set a purpose for completing the text. The student forms a question to answer alone by reading the remainder of text.
5. The student finishes reading and answers purpose-setting question(s).

Quick Tips

- When you ask questions, they should be models of good questions (those that require synthesis and evaluation as opposed to just recall).
- Ask students questions that follow up on what students have asked or that draw attention to important parts of the reading.
- Aim to connect your questions to the previously read section(s).

Question–Answer Relationship

This strategy is a variation of the QAR strategy designed by Taffy Raphael, in which answers to questions are considered to be "right there," "think and search," "author and you," or "on my own."

Purpose: This strategy assists students with understanding. They are encouraged to "read between the lines," to add what they already know to what they are being shown; sometimes the answer is not specifically in the text.

Strategy Display

Apply the QAR strategy while reading. Consider that you do not have to find the answers right in the text — you can draw on all your experiences. Relationships between questions and answers about a text can be summarized as follows:

- *What is in the text (explicit):* Is the answer found directly in the passage?
- *What is in the reader's head (implicit):* If the answer is not in the words, is it something the reader already knows? Can the reader draw upon his or her own knowledge?
- *A combination of what is in the text together with what is already known as background knowledge (explicit and implicit):* Can the answer be found both in the text *and* in the reader's own head or background knowledge?

Quick Tips

- Introduce the strategy by name.
- Discuss how it works (see above).
- Share an example, such as the following.

Question–Answer Relationships

Text: An old codger walked slowly towards the inn. He leaned heavily on his cane and bent over so that his nose pointed to the ground, almost as if the gravity was too great for him to bear. He limped slightly, dragged his left leg, and grimaced with each step.
Question: Where was he going? *to the inn*
Explicit: The answer is in the text.
Question: What is gravity? *The attraction the Earth exerts on an object on or near its surface*
Implicit: The students will rely on personal knowledge.
Question: How was he feeling? How do you know? *Leaning heavily on a cane and grimacing imply that the man was not feeling well, was perhaps tired or in pain. I know this because I have seen my grandfather stooped like this when he is hurting.*
(*Explicit and implicit:* The answer is both in the text and in students' heads.)

- Discuss how answers (or understandings) can be found in various places, including outside the text.
- Have students write
    1. text
    2. head
    3. both

in a vertical manner and then proceed to find facts to fit each category from a reading passage.

- Remind students that all written text requires the use of background knowledge as well as comprehension of the written words.
- Provide an additional passage with accompanying questions that readily fit the descriptors — text, head, both — so that students can practise the strategy.

Using Personal Knowledge

Problem: Students read (decode) well, with apparent fluency and ease, but are unable to restate or summarize in their own words what they have read.

RAP

Read
Ask
Paraphrase

Purpose: Students can *wrap* (RAP) the text ideas together by chunking and then putting what has been read into their own words.

Strategy Display

Read a chunk and stop.
Ask yourself what you just read.
Paraphrase — or, for younger students, *Put* in your own words — what you just read. Either say it to yourself or jot it down using key points.
  Continue in this way until the entire passage is read.

Quick Tips

- Discuss the strategy name and compare it to "wrap" (as in wrapping a box). Students quickly grasp how RAP and "wrap" sound alike, and note the similarities between the two actions: the RAP strategy neatly wraps up the main points of a text and presents it in one concise piece; when you wrap a gift, you tie it together and present it as a single piece.
- Discuss chunking, or breaking into smaller portions such as paragraphs, pages, or sections, if students are unfamiliar with this idea.
- Read a page or chunk together and then ask: "What did I just read?" Summarize the reading as briefly as possible.
- If students are unable to paraphrase or put in own words, reread text more slowly and try again. (Doing this prevents the all too familiar rushing ahead without understanding what is being read.)
- Provide students with options if they are still unable to paraphrase. Options include looking up unfamiliar words, looking for patterns or key words, examining titles, illustrations, or subheadings, and asking for help.

Problem: Students tend to believe explicitly in what they read — in what the words actually say. They often forget to apply their own background knowledge to aid comprehension.

Bridge
Life
Read previously
World

BRIDGE-L-R-W

Purpose: The Bridge-L-R-W strategy reminds students to better understand text or any presentation, they need to bridge, or make *connections* in three different ways: (1) to Life (L) and self, (2) to what has been Read (R) previously, and (3) to the World (W) as they know it. They call on personal background knowledge to make associations. In addition, as a visual representation, the Bridge often helps kids to better "see" what they are trying to grasp.

Strategy Display

1. Draw a small bridge on a piece of paper. It should be no more than the length of an index finger.
2. On one side of the Bridge, write or illustrate the concept or fact you do not understand or want to understand better. (Example: Why does the main character in *Looking for X* run away?)
3. On the other side, draw three lines radiating from the Bridge (see Figure 9). These will indicate Life, Read, and World.

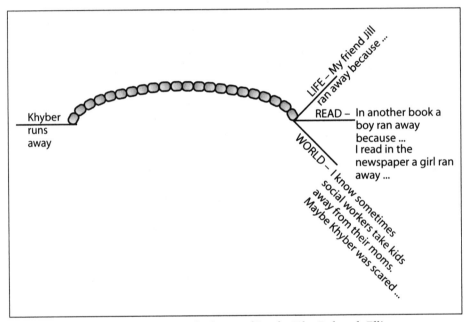

Figure 9. Bridge-L-R-W strategy applied to *Looking for X* by Deborah Ellis

4. Think of how this text (story, information) fits with your personal Life. Is the protagonist like someone you know? Where in life can you use the new information? Note this personal connection on the Life line.
5. Does this text sound like something you've Read previously? Write this on the Read line.
6. Is there something you already know about the World that helps you to understand this? Record this on the World line. If you cannot fill one of the lines, just leave it and go on.
7. Once you have created the Bridge between what you are trying to understand and what is on the other side of the Bridge, do your best to make the connections and write an explanation based on these.

Quick Tips

- The Bridge-L-R-W strategy requires some specific instruction, beginning with the purpose of a bridge (to connect two sides).
- Point out how connecting new learning to our lives, our reading, and our knowledge of the world in general can promote understanding.
- Model the strategy and invite kids to work in pairs the first time they do it.

Problem: Sometimes, kids are unable to grasp what is being presented simply because there seems to be "too much material," and they are unable to put it in context of what they already know and isolate the area of difficulty.

SAM

Simile
Analogy
Metaphor

Purpose: The SAM strategy is a comparative tool useful for instilling confidence. It lets kids see that they really can manage or handle a difficult concept or situation by comparing it to an already successfully acquired skill.

Strategy Display

1. Think of what you are trying to understand.
2. Now make a comparison between it and something you already know how to do. Develop one of the following based on whatever works best for the situation:
   - *Simile* — an explicit comparison between two different things, using "like" or "as"
   - *Analogy* — a comparison between two things that are similar in some way
   - *Metaphor* — one thing is said to be another in an imaginative, but not in a literal way
3. Tap into the powerful feelings of success associated with the already accomplished skill and transfer them to the new skill you are attempting to learn.
4. It may be helpful to break the new skill down into similar components as the learned one. Examples of SAM using each of the choices appear on the next page.

The SAM strategy is one of the most powerful tools I know of to instill confidence in kids.

Quick Tips

- Begin by discussing how students have learned a difficult skill in the past (e.g., bike riding, skating, swimming, playing a musical instrument).
- Help them to identify the steps taken when learning the specific skills, and show how these steps may be similar to learning of the new skill.
- Often, just this awareness helps kids to overcome fears and insecurities associated with learning new skills.
- If kids are not already familiar with the terms *simile, analogy,* and *metaphor,* this might be a good time to teach them. With younger students, you may want to apply the strategy and create the comparison (such as with the bike) for them. The results will still be powerful.

NEW SKILL: Multiplication

Simile: Multiplication is like adding over and over again.

NEW SKILL: Long Division

Analogy: Doing long division is just like learning to ride a bike because when you first started with a bike you had to

- focus hard
- pay close attention
- get help from someone who knew how to ride
- practise a lot
- take "baby steps"
- be very careful and watch closely what you were doing

  Now, when riding a bike, you do it automatically and are so well balanced that you can take the curves without hands on the bars. The same thing will happen with long division.

NEW SKILL: Understanding what an isosceles triangle is

Metaphor: An isosceles triangle is an icicle, long and thin with a shorter top.

SPACE

Stop
Pinpoint
Alter
Compare
Evaluate

Purpose: The SPACE strategy encourages kids to make space in their brains for something new by reminding them of already familiar steps to facilitate understanding.

Strategy Display

1. When you are having trouble understanding something, first Stop everything and take a big breath.
2. Pinpoint exactly what the problem is. What specifically do you not understand? Can you put it into a question? Is it a step in a procedure? a vocabulary word? the reason for an action?
3. Now Alter your point of view or approach to the problem. Look at it from another perspective. For example, if it is a step in a procedure, examine the steps before and after instead of focusing on the troublesome step.
4. Compare what you don't understand to what you know is similar. For the problematic step in a procedure, consider whether you have ever done a similar step somewhere else.
5. Evaluate what you have discovered during the first four steps in SPACE. Have you now been able to create some brain space? If not, repeat steps 1 and 2 and get help with the pinpointed problem.

Quick Tips

- Discuss how to create space in our brains for new information by taking the time to really understand it. (If something is not understood, it quickly disappears from the mind; hence, the lack of longevity of rote memorized facts or formula.)

- Practise each step in the SPACE strategy with kids, modelling how to, for example, Pinpoint the problem precisely. (Often kids are "stuck," but don't know where they are stuck.)
- Sometimes, just pinpointing the area of need is enough to improve understanding; if not, however, examining the situation from a different point of view may be effective. At the least, providing a plan of action removes some of the anxiety associated with not understanding.

Figuring Out Narratives

Problem: **Sometimes, even after the most enlightening follow-up discussions, it seems students still don't fully understand some specific aspect of a story. It may be something as simple as the motivation of the protagonist or as complex as the author's style of writing. They require an additional strategy for more in-depth comprehension.**

Dependent
Authorship
Writing
New

DAWN

Purpose: The DAWN strategy capitalizes on kids' natural interest in "being authors" and in embellishing what they *do* know; it asks them to contribute some *new* part of a tale "in the exact same way the author would have done this."

Strategy Display

1. Identify a specific component of the story (e.g., character motivation, roadblocks to success, description of character, sequel, or prequel).
2. Add new and exciting facts and details to the existing text. Write as if you are the author, keeping the same style as the author. Consider these ideas:

- Write a dream that the main character might have had.
- Describe a character's past experience
- Describe a change in setting due to some catastrophic event.

Quick Tips

- Discuss author style and identify some pertinent characteristics of the author in question. (For example, the author uses lots of dialogue or provides much description.)
- Point out that dawn means new start and by using the DAWN strategy, they are adding new ideas to a story. They are giving the tale a "new start," so to speak.
- Invite kids to be the author and write an expansion of the story. Explain that what they write is *dependent* on the author's style, even though they are providing new information.

Problem: **Following a narrative reading, some kids have trouble reviewing and identifying the key story elements or in understanding exactly what happened, why or how events happened, and what effects these events had on the story.**

Story Wheel

Plan to display finished Story Wheels. Kids are very proud of these.

Purpose: The Story Wheel strategy is one that kids often beg to tackle. It involves identification of and illustration of key elements on a wheel shape (see Figure 10).

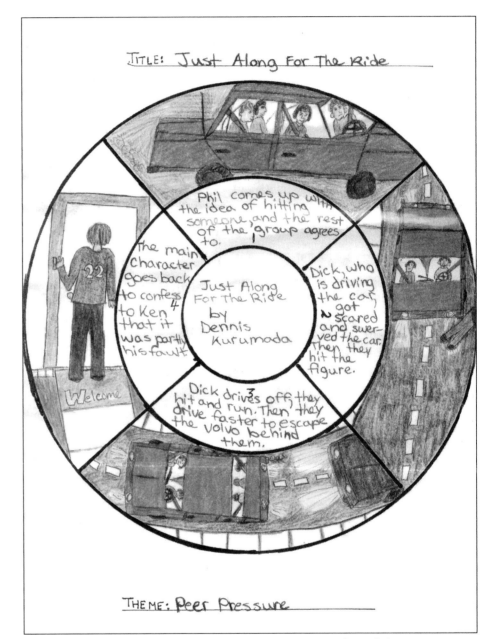

TITLE: Just Along For The Ride

Phil comes up with the idea of hitting someone, and the rest of the group agrees to.

The main character goes back to confess to Ken that it was partly his fault.

Just Along For The Ride by Dennis Kurumada

Dick, who is driving the car, got scared and swerved the car. Then they hit the figure.

Dick drives off, hit and run. Then they drive faster to escape the volvo behind them.

Welcome

22

THEME: Peer Pressure

Figure 10. Student-prepared Story Wheel: Note the clockwise flow of plot.

Strategy Display

1. Draw or work with a large circle that you have been given. There should be a small circle at the centre and two rings, the outer, of course, larger than the inner.
2. At the centre, write the name of the book or story.
3. Depending on how much text is desired, choose either the inner or the outer ring and in a sentence or phrase, record pertinent details, such as

The writing and illustrations can all be parallel to the bottom of the page or can circle the central core of the wheel. Choice is the student's.

events in the plot or protagonist traits. Typically, three to eight points are represented, and each is set off by a diagonal line through both rings.

4. In the remaining ring, illustrate the elements identified in words. For example, for a section in the inner ring that says "the car broke down on the way to camp," illustrate a car breaking down in the corresponding outer ring.

Quick Tips

- Discuss key elements, or story parts, in any narrative, pointing out that when it comes to looking at these in a specific story, readers may have different interpretations. For example, they may have different ideas on what the story theme or initial incident is.
- Discuss the key elements in a specific story, keeping in mind that some will be more significant than others. For example, in some stories the setting is relatively unimportant; in others, it makes the plot viable.
- Practise writing each element concisely.

  Element to be shown on wheel: The protagonist receives an unusual box in the mail.
  Key word interpretation: Mystery box arrives.

- Discuss how the chosen key words might be illustrated simply and effectively, for example, a brightly wrapped box with the protagonist's name on it.

BEAT

Purpose: The BEAT strategy invites kids to determine the beat of a story — that is, whether it is mainly positive or negative — by looking closely at events, their antecedents, and their outcomes.

Strategy Display

The information students come up with can be outlined in a four-column chart.

Before
Event
After
Tally

Before	Event	After	Tally

1. Determine the important, or key, events in the narrative (Event column).
2. For each event, determine what happened before it; think about what might have caused it (Before column).
3. Determine what happened immediately after each event (After column); tie this to the "Before."
4. Determine the event's effect on the story as a whole. Tally the positive or negative value of each event (Tally column).

Quick Tips

- Discuss the idea of events, or roadblocks, in narratives, and how some have positive effects while others have negative effects. Together, identify these in a narrative.

- Discuss the concept of a tally (a reckoning or scoring) of positive and negative occurrences, and what effects these can have on a protagonist. Draw out authentic occurrences from the classroom: for example, when the fire alarm (event) went off right before Physical Education and the class had to miss most of the class (negative tally), the result was unhappy kids.
- Present the concept of finding the *beat* of the story. Is the beat largely negative or positive? This angle is a little different from the usual connotation of "beat," but kids quickly understand and accept it, and enjoy using the BEAT strategy.

PLAN

Problem
Lesson
Action
Nature

Purpose: The PLAN strategy is a simple reminder for kids to examine narratives for four basic components, identification of which will help clarify the story.

Strategy Display

Determine each of the following:

- the Problem that the main character faced
- the Lesson, or moral, the narrative included
- the Action the main character took
- the Nature, or approach, of the story: Was it happy? scary? mysterious? sad?

Quick Tips

- Discuss the PLAN strategy by comparing it to a *plan* used by an author when writing.
- Discuss the problem and action of the main character. Helping kids figure out what action the main character takes when presented with a problem also helps with comprehension.
- Every narrative has, to some degree, a lesson, given explicitly or implicitly in the content. Helping kids find this lesson or moral helps them better understand narrative.
- Discuss how stories differ in the way they make us feel. Refer to this as the Nature of the narrative, and connect to PLAN by pointing out that authors *plan* to make us experience certain emotions when we read their work and that the Nature of the narrative is suggested by the "N" in PLAN.

4-S

Someone
Situation
Setting
Self

Purpose: The 4-S strategy is a useful tool to remind kids about story conflict: it suggests that conflict can be between a main character and different oppositions, and thus increases comprehension of the story.

Strategy Display

1. Consider whether the main character is being opposed by

   - Someone (another person)
   - a Situation (something happening in the protagonist's life)

- a Setting (the protagonist's physical or emotional world)
- Self (protagonist in conflict with self, as in conscience)

2. Write the protagonist's name on one line and draw an arrow connecting the name to the most serious type of opposition faced — to one of the "S's" in the 4-S strategy.

3. If the character is opposed by more than one "S," put the appropriate "S's" under the first, ranking them. You thereby show that the first "S" listed has the most effect on the character, with subsequent "S's" having less effect.

4. In a few words, tell why you have chosen each "S." (See boxed example.)

5. Write briefly about any remaining "S's," explaining why you think they are not in opposition to the character. Write them as "Not an opposition."

Opposition the Protagonist Faces

Setting: Storm in which protagonist is lost — the storm is an antagonist.

Self: Doesn't have confidence in himself, so Self tends to work as an antagonist — he is in conflict with Self.

Situation: He must reach his cousin's home to warn him of an impending problem — the Situation becomes an antagonist as he is naturally worried about his inability to reach the destination.

Not an opposition: Someone — no one else is in the story.

---

6. Once the 4-S strategy has been employed and the type of conflict discovered, move on to determining the other details of the story.

Quick Tips

- Discuss the various types of conflict with students, using examples from their reading.
- Once kids understand the idea of conflict, comprehension of the rest of the story is often improved.

P-L

Plot
Line

Purpose: The P-L strategy invites kids to create a visual representation of the sequence of events in a story, thereby aiding in understanding of cause and effect, character motivation, and story resolution.

Strategy Display

1. Pick the key elements from the story: these include setting, initial incident, roadblocks, rising action incidents, highest point of action, climax, and resolution.

2. Draw a line to illustrate the upward movement to the climax.

3. Mark the various points along the line. (See Figure 11.)

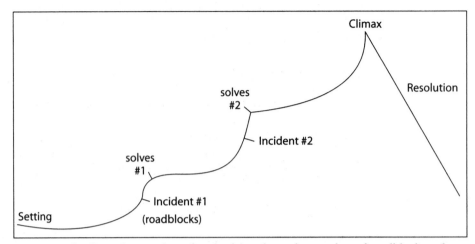

Figure 11. Plot line: The number of peaks depends on the number of roadblocks to be dealt with.

4. You may wish to illustrate each point. In that case, you are making a story map. (See Figure 12.)

Figure 12. Story map for *Freak the Mighty*, prepared by a student

Quick Tips

- Begin by teaching or discussing story grammar (the names of the various component of a story, such as setting and initial incident).
- Model a plot line. Create one together from a shared narrative.
- Allow individualization when creating plot lines as each student will view the story according to individual perceptions. There is no right or wrong way to do this.

- Display finished work, especially if students have taken the extra step to make the plot lines into story maps.

S-T-S

Sketch-To-Stretch

This strategy is suggested for group or partner work, but can also be done independently. See suggestions in Quick Tips.

Purpose: The Sketch-To-Stretch strategy, one of the familiar strategies included in this book, helps students better understand the story elements and their connections; it puts emphasis on students' ideas and feelings, not on their artistic abilities.

Strategy Display

1. Read a story (shared reading or independent) and discuss.
2. Brainstorm ways to represent or illustrate the story (lines, shapes, colors, images).
3. In small groups or partners, makes sketches of the story meaning, as you see it. Draw how you feel about a scene — there is no right or wrong way to do this.
4. Share sketches with peers and discuss what you think others are trying to say.
5. Revise sketches and make final copies, if you wish.

Quick Tips

- Review or teach story elements.
- Discuss various ways to illustrate, including use of lines (e.g., sharp, jagged lines vs. soft curving lines), shapes, colors (bright vs. pastel; shades and tints), abstracts, symbols, or more literal representations.
- Let students know that there is no right or wrong way to illustrate feelings and that probably no two people will have the same reaction to any story. The purpose of this strategy is to allow everyone to share a variety of feelings and responses.
- Students can use the S-T-S strategy independently by reading, illustrating their thoughts/reactions, reading further, illustrating again, and so on. In this way, they keep a record of their emotions as they "stretch," or go through changes.

Making Sense of Text

Problem: **Text can be arranged or structured in so many ways that sometimes students, confused by what they see and perhaps expecting a familiar form, miss important points. They may be unable to sort out what is important from what is less important, and to isolate, paraphrase, or summarize these elements.**

C & E

Cause & Effect

This strategy is familiar, but the two suggested orientations of the chart may be different.

Purpose: The C & E strategy is a visual representation of things that occur and their results. It works equally well for narrative or expository text.

Strategy Display

Simple structure for younger students

1. Draw two or three boxes in a vertical column on the left side of the page.
2. Put the word "cause" in each box.
3. Depending on the number of "effects" for each cause, draw one or more line(s) radiating from each box.
4. Draw boxes at the end of each of the lines radiating out from the "cause" boxes and briefly write or illustrate the effects (see Figure 13).

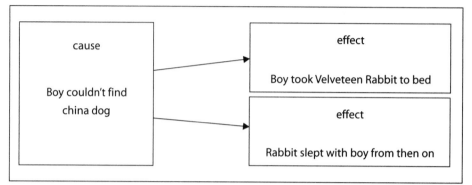

Figure 13. Example of a simple C & E structure applied to *The Velveteen Rabbit* by Margery Williams

More complex, event-based structure

This form of C & E helps students to better understand both the reasons for a major event and its repercussions.

1. Draw a single box in the centre of the page. Write the word "event" in it and then identify a major happening in the story or piece of informative text.
2. Draw one or more boxes to the left of the centre box, and join them to the centre with lines. In each box, record a cause of the event. In the case of *Looking for X* by Deborah Ellis, the event of the protagonist getting lost is associated with these causes: the protagonist, Khyber, is unfairly accused of vandalism; Khyber's mother doesn't believe her; and Khyber sets out to seek X, a street friend.
3. Draw enough boxes on the right side of the centre box to equal the number of effects related to the main event identified there. For example, effects of Khyber getting lost are that her mother panics, Khyber cries, and Khyber meets a group of female Elvises (see Figure 14).

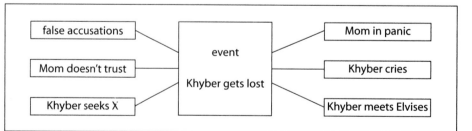

Figure 14. This chart shows causes and effects of Khyber getting lost, which is the central event in *Looking for X*.

Written explanations of any of the stages (cause, event, or effect) can be replaced by illustrations. For example, instead of writing "Khyber cries," the student could draw a picture of the girl crying. Students do not have to take only one approach for all boxes; they should be able to write or illustrate according to what works best for them.

4. All of these key points have been pulled out of the story; the same process can be applied to expository text. The "facts" that are shown as the effects can then be viewed as further causes. For example, Khyber meeting the Elvises can be viewed as a cause with the effects that they console her, escort her home, and help the family find a new home.
5. For each event identified, go through the same process of determining causes and effects. Remember that a single event may have several causes and several effects associated with it.

Quick Tips

- Discuss cause and effect in daily life. "Being late for school is an event. Think backwards and see if you can identify a cause. If the cause of the lateness was your alarm clock not going off, that would appear in a box on the left. The effects of the event might include missing something important in class, having a detention for being late, or disrupting the class."
- Point out how these effects can then become causes of further events and effects. For example, the effect missing something important in class might, in turn, become the cause of failing a test. Once kids realize that causes and effects usually have this domino effect, invite them to use the C & E strategy to closely examine information.
- Follow-up discussion can help with understanding of how causes become effects and so on. For example, the alarm clock cause leads to the late-for-school effect. The missing breakfast effect leads to feeling hungry, which becomes a cause of the effect of being irritable, and so on.

P & S

Problem & **S**olution

Again, this strategy is familiar; it is the chart labelling that differs.

The idea, developed by creative Grade 6 kids, is that a problem is sad, but a solution is happy. Anything that encourages kids to better understand what they are reading works for me!

Purpose: Similar to the C & E strategy, the P & S strategy is a visual depiction of problems and what happens to solve them.

Strategy Display

1. Divide the page vertically. Put the word "Problem," top left, and "Solution," top right. (Or, use simple faces: one unsmiling, one smiling.)

Both the C & E and P & S strategies can be represented in many forms; every teachers' guide will offer a variety of these. The simplest form, however, is the double-entry page used here.

2. Locate as many problems from the text as you can, keeping in mind that some problems may not be explicitly part of the text. You may have to use your judgment.
3. Record each problem on the left side.
4. Now, on the right side, provide a solution for each problem. Again, the solution may not be explicitly written. You may have to guess or devise it, based on what you know and what you have read.

Quick Tips

- Discuss problems and solutions in daily life by starting with a class problem. Discuss possible solutions.
- Introduce the P & S strategy and if using, the happy/sad faces.
- Encourage kids to "think between the lines," to tap into what they already know and link to previous knowledge. Doing this promotes better understanding.
- Consider the appropriateness of other variations on the P & S (or C & E) theme. A few are outlined below in Figure 15.

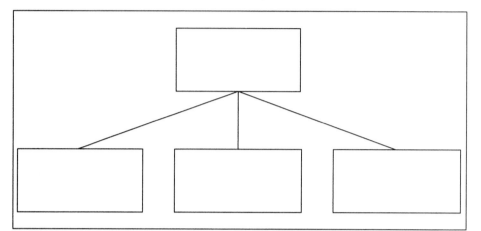

Figure 15. Variations on P & S (or C & E) shown as graphic organizers
A. The problem or cause appears at the top and the solutions or effects are outlined below.

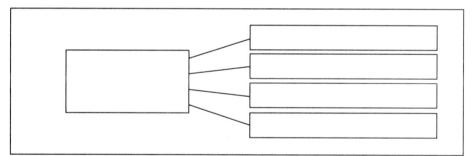

B. Either a problem or a cause appears in a bubble at left; solutions or effects appear to the right.

STEPS

Purpose: The Steps strategy is a visual depiction of the key elements in a longer piece of writing, such as a novel; it can also be used for expository writing. This "teacher favorite" strategy not only encourages kids to summarize chapters or sections, but also provides proof that they have completed the required reading.

Strategy Display

1. The goal of the Steps strategy is to show the development of a narrative or informative piece from beginning to end, so begin at the bottom left corner and draw the first step (see Figure 16).
2. In the step, print key words or phrases about the first chapter or section. Basically, you are providing a brief chapter summary. Note as well the

effect of the events on the protagonist. (For example, for Chapter 3 in *Looking for X*, you could say that Khyber is worried.)

3. After reading the next chapter or section, draw the second step and follow the same procedure.

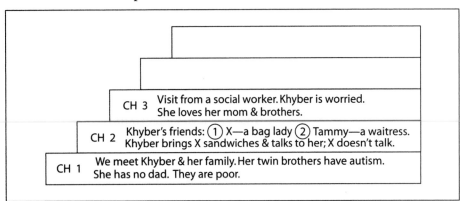

Figure 16. Steps strategy applied to *Looking for X* by Deborah Ellis, first three chapters

To use Steps with expository text, think of each step as a representation of either a chapter summary or important points within a chapter.

4. When you reach the top of the steps, you should be at the end of the book. If you run out of space on the page, begin where you left off on another page, bottom left.

Quick Tips

- Share an illustration of what the Steps strategy will look like when finished or partially finished.
- Discuss how to determine the key elements in a chapter (or shorter section if you wish), and how to print these neatly in a step.
- Discuss how the elements affect the protagonist. Brainstorm for emotional description words. Point out that sometimes the effects are physical, too. (For example, the protagonist suffers a broken arm due to some incident in the chapter.)
- Point out that the Steps strategy is an ongoing strategy that will be finished only when the student has completed the text.
- Some kids like to include small illustrations in or on their steps as well as the writing. Encourage individuality.
- This strategy is a great pre–book report activity, as it encourages constant evaluation and summarization. In so doing, it is also an aid to comprehension.
- Although mostly used for narratives, Steps can be used with informational text. Each step can represent a chapter or section summary, questions related to chapters or sections, or key points from chapters or sections.

MAP

Most
Affect
Pinpoint

Purpose: The MAP strategy is a simple tool to help with identification of main ideas and key words or elements in sentences or paragraphs, in any form of text.

Strategy Display

In order to figure out what a sentence or paragraph is really all about, ask yourself the following three questions.

- What is the Most important idea? (This is the one idea that stands out, the one that is the basis of all other ideas or words.)
- How would removal of this idea or the words that express it Affect the rest of the sentence or paragraph? (If you remove them, the rest should not make sense.)
- What words can you write to Pinpoint this sentence or paragraph? In other words, how can you draw specific attention to the main idea in a sentence or paragraph in as few words as possible through a summary using the selected words?

Think of this as a skeleton *map* or overview of the sentence or paragraph, much like a map showing landforms.

Quick Tips

- Discuss key points, elements, or words, probably a review of some sort.
- Introduce the MAP strategy by drawing connections to the acronym and a topographical *map*. (Both show the most important parts: not every small detail or every little hill.)
- Help kids to identify key components of a piece of text as single words or short phrases. For example, consider the sentence "As I opened the trap door, I peered in to see not just a single, trembling, furry mouse looking back at me, but also five, tiny, hairless, pink infant mice lying on the bare metal floor of the trap." It can be condensed, or Pinpointed, into "A mother and five baby mice were in the trap." The Most important points include "mother, five babies, mice, and trap." Removal of any of these words Affects the sentence so that it no longer makes sense.
- Use cloze activities to help reinforce the concept of key points.
- While using the MAP strategy, discuss the difference between *affect* and *effect*.

Focusing Attention

Problem: **Some kids, often the weaker readers, have considerable difficulty understanding the general content of both narrative and expository text. They struggle with decoding and then struggle even more so with comprehension. They can't focus well enough to tell you what they have "read."**

T-G-I-F

Purpose: The T-G-I-F strategy is a quick reminder to use the context to gain clues about a reading before you begin. T-G-I-F provides a framework for better comprehension.

Strategy Display

1. Before beginning to read, look at the Title and make a prediction.
2. Next, determine the Genre, or kind of written work. Is the piece narrative or expository? Is it science fiction, adventure, myth or legend, fairy tale, romance, historical fiction? Is it a news report, a persuasive article, a textbook summary? What are its distinctive characteristics?

Title
Genre
Illustrations
Form

I always use T-G-I-F before purchasing a novel; I carry out the scan automatically.

3. Closely examine any accompanying Illustrations — in the case of a novel, the book jacket or cover — and try to get an idea as to content.
4. Determine the Form. For the purpose of this strategy, *form* refers to the point of view and organization of the piece and considers questions like these: From whose point of view is the story written? (Is it in first, second, or third person or possibly from the point of view of an inanimate object or animal?) How is the story organized? For example, does it begin with dialogue or with high action? Does it use flashbacks? If it is expository, how is it organized? Is it a sequenced representation of facts? Is it structured for cause and effect, pro and con, problem and solution, or enumeration?

Quick Tips

- Discuss how to use context clues for quick information.
- Together, look at a few book covers and make predictions.
- Discuss the genre and illustrations and draw comparisons between narrative and expository writing. (In both cases, T-G-I-F is highly effective.)

DED

Double
Entry
Data

Purpose: The DED strategy encourages students to focus on what they are reading by prompting them to write questions and responses about it in a journal.

Strategy Display

1. Draw a vertical line down a page.
2. On the left side, write questions, queries, and concerns about what you are reading.
3. When you have finished reading, return to each item on the left side; on the right side, write a comment, such as "Still don't understand" or "Now, I see that means . . ."
4. For left-side entries you still don't understand, reread the section or get help before proceeding.

Quick Tips

- Discuss how writing things down often helps with understanding.
- Model the DED strategy, using a shared text and simulating your questions.
- Demonstrate how to reread for more information about left-side entries not understood.

K-W-L

Know
Want
Learned

Purpose: The familiar K-W-L strategy involves the students in active thinking by asking them to stimulate prior knowledge about the subject to be studied or read. It encourages focus and concentration on the topic.

Strategy Display

1. Divide a page into three columns, and write at the top these column heads:

K (Know)	W (Want to know)	L (Learned)

2. Before reading, listening, or viewing a certain text, consider the general theme or content and fill in the left and middle columns of the chart.
3. After reading, listening, or viewing, fill in the right column.

Quick Tips

- Because this is such a familiar strategy, little needs to be said. Just remember to allow for a wide variety of responses in each column.
- Discuss how to activate prior knowledge (listed in the Know column) by looking at titles and illustrations, and by reading the opening and closing sentences for prompts. Encourage students to let these prompts bring to mind everything they already know about what they are going to read.
- Invite students to find ways to discover information about anything written in the Want to know column not yet resolved.

THINK-A-LOUD

Purpose: Think-A-Loud helps kids to construct meaning from text by speaking their thoughts out loud, in a controlled manner; it also focuses attention.

Strategy Display

If students are practising the strategy in class, a whisper is accepted.

1. Read silently until you come to something that makes you think, query, wonder, or react.
2. Whisper the question or comment to yourself; if you raised a question, then quietly attempt to answer it.
3. Continue reading and talking to yourself as you go.

Quick Tips

- This is a wonderful strategy for aiding comprehension, but kids will probably react negatively to the idea of "talking out loud" while reading. (We have done such a good job of instilling silent reading!) Point out to them that whispered self-talk is OK.
- Model how to think aloud. In the example below, the italicized type represents the teacher pausing in her reading aloud of the text to reflect.

> *The Three Questions*, based on a story by Leo Tolstoy, by Jon J. Muth:
>
> "Remember that there is only one important time, and that time is now. *(Gee, that makes me think of how every minute is important.)* The most important one is always the one you are with. *(Hmmm. What if I don't like the one I'm with? Is that person still the most important? I guess maybe at that particular time . . .)* And the most important thing to do is to do good for the one who is standing at your side. *(OK. What if I don't know how to do that? This is a tough idea.)* For these, my dear boy, are the answers to what is most important in this world. *(Well, I'm not sure if I agree with that last sentence, but this author has made me think . . .)*

6

Creating

Creativity is more than just the ability to use the imagination to be original in thought and action; it is also the capacity to be resourceful, to think divergently, and to exhibit ingenuity — important traits for successful living. For some people, creativity seems serendipitous. To them, the generation of novel ideas appears natural and spontaneous. We all know someone who seems to exude creativity from every pore. For others, however, creativity represents a great deal of good old-fashioned hard work. We are familiar with these people too — the plunderers and plodders who occasionally seem to produce an amazing idea. Teachers have students in both categories and everywhere in between. For this reason, they need to share as many strategies for stimulating those "creative juices" as possible. Some strategies tie directly to the project or situation at hand; others provide an avenue for non-specific creative ideas to be generated, sort of like "exercises for the creativity section of the brain."

We associate the right side of the brain with emotions, imagination, and creativity and the left side with logical thought and analysis. To achieve better creative results, we need to give time to both left-brain and right-brain activities; however, research suggests that if we keep bouncing back and forth between creative and analytical activities, we'll probably end up with headaches instead of creative ideas. The solution, if there is one, is to focus completely on one "side of the brain," on either logic or creativity, for enough time as is needed to reach some sort of conclusion or closure. If we are trying to be creative, as we are discussing in this part of the book, it helps to put away logical thought for a time — a few minutes or a few hours — depending on the nature of the task. That's why strategies such as those offered in this chapter tend to suspend judgment while ideas are being created.

Whether decorating a basement bachelor suite or a penthouse, dressing for high fashion or a football game, setting a table for one or 100, or selecting the best dish from a fast-food franchise or a fine dining establishment, creativity is involved. Creativity is also part of communication. Whether writing a text message to a peer or an article for a professional magazine, speaking to five people or 50, listening to a senior or to an orchestra, divergent thinking is required.

It would be impossible to survive without at least a moderate degree of innovativeness and creative thinking. In fact, the ability to be creative in life refers more to being productive, inspired, and capable than to being imaginative and innovative. Happily, to some degree, students can be taught these traits through strategies, such as those presented in this chapter.

Sigmund Freud suggested that creativity was the result of frustration and emotional tension. Certainly, teachers know when their students are experiencing these negative emotions when in pursuit of that perfect and elusive "creative" idea. In such cases, teachers can help students by teaching them strategies, such as BOB, so that they will not *have* to experience frustration when trying to come up with that perfect idea.

J. P. Guilford, on the other hand, suggested that creativity was the result of divergent thinking and the consequent innovative generation of multiple answers to a set problem. With this understanding in mind, teachers can encourage and empower divergent thinking by sharing strategies with their students. They want their students to be able to produce many choices and select the best ones with, occasionally, extraordinary results. Often a strategy, such as Star or POP (see pages 92 and 93), will facilitate this.

How often do teachers hear that their students can't think of anything to write, draw, build, or say? This is a sure sign that a creativity-inducing strategy is called for.

Blasting Mental Blocks

Problem: **A major problem faced by kids of all ages is coming up with novel ideas either for writing, speaking, or illustrative purposes. It seems it's all been said or done before. They are left feeling blocked, or "stuck." They don't realize that ideas can come at many different times during the day and be recalled when needed.**

CUD

Purpose: The wonderful CUD strategy serves to mindfully stimulate creative thought during the many moments of downtime we all have daily.

Careful
Use of
Downtime

This strategy I utilize constantly when writing a book, and it never fails me.

An alternative way to use CUD is to consciously get away from a problem by not thinking of it, by doing something else, possibly physical, such as going for a walk, and allowing ideas to sift at random through your mind. This use of downtime is effective for many.

Strategy Display

1. Recognize when you are having downtime (see Quick Tips below).
2. Consciously focus your mind on a problem to be solved or a "creation" you want to produce.
3. Keep thinking about the problem or hoped-for creation all through the downtime, paying attention to the many random thoughts that will race through your mind.
4. Jot down ideas immediately or as soon as possible following.

Quick Tips

- Discuss *downtime* as time when we are physically involved in tasks that take little mental effort. Brainstorm for as many of these occasions as possible. The list may include walking a dog or going to or from school; sitting in a car, bus, or plane; waiting in line; and doing chores.
- Discuss what we normally think of during these times. (Many kids won't remember; downtime is literally "wasted brain time.")
- Discuss what cows do when chewing their *cud* — basically nothing — and draw the connection between strategy name and downtime so that kids will better remember the strategy for future use.
- Discuss how to focus personal attention on an existing situation, such as something they want to write about. Suggestions for doing this include the following:
  - Slow down by taking a few deep breaths.
  - For 10 breaths, think of your breathing only.

- Now, think of the problem or situation, but do so in positive terms. Instead of "I hate writing essays and I have one due on Friday," say to yourself: "By writing this essay, I can improve my writing skills."
- Train your brain to stop useless chatter — the rapid moving away from the problem to other, more pleasant pursuits. As soon as your mind starts to do this, mentally stop the thought flow and return it to the problem at hand.
- Invite students to practise CUD on their way home from school and to record any ideas they come up with.
- You may wish to remind students that focusing of any kind becomes more difficult if they are fatigued; encourage them to get adequate sleep.

Caution: Advise students against using CUD before sleep. This strategy is a stimulation activity and will inhibit sleep.

BOB

Breathe
Open-mind
Brainstorm

Purpose: The BOB strategy provides a set of directions for tapping into personal creativity.

Strategy Display

Similar to the CUD strategy, BOB can best be utilized during downtime; however, it can be employed at any time when you want to think creatively. So, when you need to focus on the topic or concern about which you wish to think creatively, begin by breathing deeply and slowly several times.

1. Breathe in and formulate the concern in your mind.
2. Breathe out and try to think of nothing — open your mind.
3. Repeat this in-focus–out-open pattern three to six times.
4. Stop the deep breathing and focus on the concern, allowing your mind to bounce randomly around. Pay attention to the creative thoughts that flit into your consciousness and quickly jot ideas down.
5. When you have run out of ideas, repeat from the beginning, if desired.

Quick Tips

- Practise the strategy together.
- Be aware that although this strategy may seem easy, putting effort into it can be quite exhausting. Often, once through the steps is enough to stimulate a number of creative thoughts; however, if one set of in-focus–out-open, repeated three to six times, doesn't bring any ideas, don't pursue it further at this time.

P-P-G

Play
Personal
Games

Purpose: The P-P-G strategy encourages kids to stretch their imaginations by playing personal games during downtime periods, and in so doing, enhance their creativity in general.

Strategy Display

1. Identify when you are having downtime (see page 90).
2. Look around and let your eyes focus on anything — a cup, a door, an umbrella, a tree, a cell phone.
3. Begin thinking of all the things or actions that object could be used for other than that for which it is intended (e.g., a cup for a goldfish bowl,

for a growing plant, for a hat, for a chain hung around the neck, for an eye mask or ear muff). Be as silly as possible.

4. Keep thinking until you can't come up with another single thing. Be sure to laugh at yourself.

Quick Tips

- Discuss the problems with trying to be creative.
- Suggest that creativity, like other mental functions such as memory, can be trained.
- Suggest that P-P-G is a simple way to stimulate creativity.
- Together, go through the steps using some common classroom object.

After doing P-P-G, kids may choose to work on a writing or illustrating project.

Expanding Existing Ideas

Problem: **Students often find it difficult to embellish or make bigger a single idea for creative endeavors.**

STAR

Purpose: Star is a visual strategy that stimulates creativity by encouraging recall or discovery of alternative words while also encouraging brainstorming on topic.

Strategy Display

1. Begin by drawing a vertical line on a page.
2. At one end, print a word or short phrase related to the subject.
3. At the opposite end, print a word that is either a synonym or an antonym of the first word. If you record a synonym, this will show another similar idea; an antonym will remind you of an opposing position to include in your presentation, writing, or visualization.
4. Draw an intersecting line and repeat the word-printing. You may show antonyms and synonyms within the same star.
5. Continue this procedure with intersecting lines until you have created a full star. Remember to put words on the Star points. (See Figure 17.)

Hint: Make each line a different length so that there is room to print.

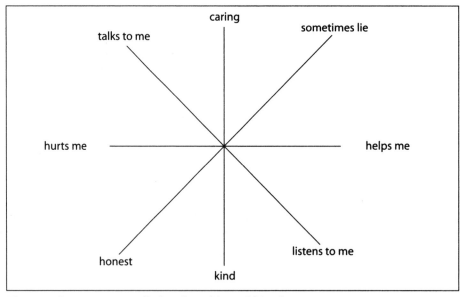

Figure 17. Star strategy applied to the subject of friends

6. Use the ideas from the Star to proceed with your project.

Quick Tips

- Share a completed Star, pointing out how to make lines intersect and how to vary line lengths.
- Discuss how or where to find synonyms or antonyms if they are not known.
- Discuss how to use these synonyms or antonyms in the final creation.
- Encourage keeping of the stars and handing in with completed assignments as "Creation pages."

POP

Pen
On
Paper

Help from POP
I will never forget the Grade 4 student who called to me in the hall, "Teacher, I got a great story idea using POP last night." I knew what he meant; we had just learned the POP strategy. However, a listening peer said to me, "Isn't that great he's getting help from his father." I smiled, but said nothing.

Purpose: The POP strategy encourages kids to let their ideas *pop* by using a free flow pen technique.

Strategy Display

1. Get a fresh piece of lined paper.
2. Put your pen or pencil on the first line and just start writing on any topic. If you can't get started, simply write about what you see around you. This may stimulate you to write about other topics too. If you have a specific topic about which to write, start by writing the word or words of that topic and see what happens. If, after five minutes, you haven't written anything, ask if you can change the topic.
3. Write whatever comes to mind, not stopping for sentences, grammar, spelling, or anything.
4. Keep your pen on the paper and write until you have at least half a page filled with words, thoughts, phrases, and ideas.
5. Return to the start. Circle or highlight the best ideas for writing correctly or for using in visual art.

Quick Tips

- Discuss ways to "be creative" and introduce the POP strategy. Explain that it will help ideas to *pop*.
- Demonstrate. Examples might look something like these:

    Topic: Writing about friends
    Friends are fun help you do not bully funny always listen do not tell you bad stuff go to the park phone you homework likes me

    Topic: Creating a poster about pollution
    Dirty air too much cars on the road poor air lots of garbage big clouds of smoke people coughing red cross sick people hospitals dead fish

- Practise choosing the best ideas from the POP activity.

ALPHABET

Employing the Alphabet strategy for creativity is an old ploy, but still useful.

Purpose: Kids focus on each letter of the alphabet in sequence, thinking of words (or images) that begin with each and relate to a problem/situation to create a bank of connected ideas.

Strategy Display

1. Focus on the problem at hand.
2. Think of a word that begins with the letter "A" and relates to the topic.
   Sample topic for writing: Technology
   A   assess (activate, autoformat)
3. Continue through the entire alphabet. If some letters do not lead to a word, ignore them and continue; if some letters provide more than one word — great!
   You may wish to use a dictionary to help stimulate ideas.
   B   Blackberry (break, bullets)
   C   computer (customize, clear)
   D   data (delete, document)
   And so on.
4. Once you have completed the alphabet, review your words. Use the good ones; delete the not-so-good ones, or save them just in case they later "fit."

Quick Tips

- Discuss the importance of being creative when writing or producing visual art.
- Discuss the Alphabet strategy and practise it together.

CAVE

Purpose: The CAVE strategy invites kids to seek an inner mind-picture and brightly reproduce it whether in written or representational form.

Create A Vibrant Example

Strategy Display

1. Close your eyes and imagine you are in a cave that you consider safe and cozy.
2. Now focus on the area or idea you wish to reproduce. Think of the general theme and let your mind wander at will. Examples of general themes are friends/friendships, autumn, happiness, pets, and family.
3. You "see" that one wall in the cave is lit like a big movie screen, and on that screen, beautiful pictures begin to form. Create the most amazing mental pictures you can.
4. "Watch" the pictures form and change. Choose the one you like best — the most Vibrant Example — and really focus on it.
5. Let that special picture stay on the cave wall screen until you have memorized all the details: the colors, shapes, textures, lines, and so on.
6. In your mind, walk out of the cave with the detailed picture firmly in your head.
7. Begin writing or drawing immediately, referring often to the mind-picture you have created. If you forget some of the details, return to the cozy cave and watch the "show" again.

Quick Tips

- Not all students will be able to use this highly creative strategy, but those who do use it generally get amazing results. Respect individual differences by not insisting that all students use CAVE.
- Introduce the concept of a cave. Keep the discussion geared towards a warm, beautiful, cozy cave as opposed to a dark, damp, scary one (unless, of course, you wish the result to be a scary depiction, as in a Halloween tale or illustration).
- Discuss the CAVE strategy, talking about the meaning of the word "vibrant" and brainstorming words that show vibrancy.

A-L-B-M

A
Little
Bit
More

Purpose: The A-L-B-M strategy encourages kids to keep going, to think of, or to provide *A Little Bit More* — to in some way stretch what they are working on.

Strategy Display

1. Focus on what you are trying to create, perhaps a written, visual, or oral depiction.
2. Once you have figured out how to creatively show it, stop and use the A-L-B-M strategy. Force yourself to

   - add more ideas
   - use different words
   - expand your thoughts
   - make it bigger, better, more convincing

3. Continue to use A-L-B-M for at least 10 minutes; then, rethink your position, illustration, or writing, adding the new ideas.
4. If you are still not satisfied, stop and use A-L-B-M again to really expand your ideas. Remember: A-L-B-M is a "s t r e t c h i n g" strategy. Refuse to be satisfied with the first attempt.

Quick Tips

- Introduce the A-L-B-M strategy as a personal effort to get more from oneself by insisting on a little bit more.
- Consider tying the A-L-B-M strategy to the idea of physical stretching where, with constant practice, the body will stretch more. Or, tie it to the concept of a coach constantly asking for a little bit more of athletes or sports teams. Discuss what happens when athletes are constantly encouraged to give a little bit more.
- Encourage daily use of the A-L-B-M strategy in as many areas as possible (e.g., when writing, doing a mathematics problem, reading a text, or practising a skill).

Problem: **Even the most creative students sometimes forget to use all the possible avenues open to them, the most obvious being their five senses.**

S-IT

Purpose: S-It reminds kids to make full use of their senses when thinking creatively.

Strategy Display

- Sit calmly and go through each of your senses individually, connecting each to the situation or problem at hand. In other words, how can each sense affect the situation? Follow this order:
    1. Sight
    2. Smell
    3. Hearing
    4. Touch
    5. Taste
- Keep a record of the effect of each sense.

Quick Tips

- Review the senses with students. Use a specific object (a piece of fruit or a rock) and invite kids to discuss each sense with a partner.
- Encourage creative responses: "The rock smells damp and musty."
- Encourage *expansion* of the initial statement(s): "The rock, buried for centuries in a grave, was recently dug up by a dog looking for a bone."
- Point out that sometimes (as with taste), we might have only our imaginations to draw on — that is creative thought.

Stepping Away from the Ordinary

Problem: **For some kids, it's difficult to "think outside the box," to play what if, to move away from the ordinary, or to escape into fantasy. It seems the older students get, the less able they are to do this. Teachers need to use as many strategies as possible to help students improve their imaginative and creative thinking.**

K-C 1, 2, 3

Purpose: K-C 1, 2, 3 invites kids to be creative by avoiding commonplace clichés, using one of three possible alternatives.

Strategy Display

Instead of using a cliché, try one of the following options:

Cliché: As quiet as a mouse

1. Change the words to synonyms, making use of a thesaurus:

    as hushed as a small rodent hiding from a cat

Sense-
It

I once had a student tell me that the pinkish rock I held in my hand "tasted like candy floss." Creative! And who's to say it didn't taste like candy floss?

Kill
Clichés
1, 2, 3

2. Rewrite the cliché as a paragraph:

> He was so silent, his steps so soft — almost as if he was trying to avoid the attention of some terrible monster. Not a sound he made, not even that of gentle breathing. He was so subdued that not a soul heard him approach.

3. Take the "opposite" approach: express the idea using a negative combined with the opposite of what the cliché implies:

> was certainly not noisy, loud, or raucous

Quick Tips

- Discuss clichés and how they kill creativity.
- Brainstorm some common clichés as a class and follow the K-C 1, 2, 3 strategy together.

WATCH

What
Alternative
Thing
Could
Happen

Purpose: The WATCH strategy allows for tapping into the wildest possible thoughts and ideas related to something common and familiar. It encourages extremes of thinking; there are no limitations, no *rights* or *wrongs*.

Strategy Display

1. Randomly examine (watch) a familiar object, situation, animal, or even person, while asking yourself "What alternative thing could happen if . . . ?"
2. Mentally finish this question with whatever thoughts come to mind.
3. Now, brainstorm as many answers to the created question as possible. Remember that there are no wrong answers.
4. Keep jot notes or illustrations of the ideas for future use.

Quick Tips

- Discuss the concept of random thought. (There are no guidelines to the thinking; it can be bizarre.)
- Point out how the strategy specifically states alternative things; discuss the meaning of the word "alternative."
- Do the WATCH strategy as a class with some familiar object, for example, a pen.

  > Question: "What alternative thing could happen if this pen talked?"
  > It might say: "Please turn me right side up. All the ink is running to my head and giving me a headache."
  > It might beg to write a letter to its friend the pencil.
  > It might ask never to be put into a backpack again because it is afraid of the dark.

- Demonstrate how to use jot notes or illustrations to keep a record of the ideas.
- Tell kids that this strategy reminds us to *watch* closely for unusual and creative ideas daily. There is never a moment during a day when it would not be possible to use WATCH.

**Magic
Minute**

M-M fits well into the pre-writing stage of the writing process.

True, the strategy often takes longer than a minute to apply, but the notion of it taking only a Magic Minute to get a great idea appeals to kids. I recall a sweet young girl in Grade 4 who had been sitting with wrinkled brow for about the first 15 minutes of a writing period. When I questioned what she was doing, she replied, "Well, my Magic Minute has lasted for a whole lot longer, but I think I finally got it!"

Purpose: The M-M strategy serves to quickly and effectively stimulate "weird and wonderful" ideas. It gives kids permission to be unrealistic and fanciful as a preparatory stage to creative writing, representation, or improvising a dramatic skit.

Strategy Display

1. Focus on the task at hand (e.g., a writing or drawing project).
2. Tell yourself that for the next 60 seconds, you are going to let your imagination run wild.
3. Now, begin the M-M countdown. Watch the classroom clock and really fantasize or think in wildly imaginative ways for 60 seconds.

If nothing comes to mind, repeat the M-M strategy. You can repeat it again and again until you get that wonderful idea right there to be claimed.

Quick Tips

- Discuss the problems we all have in trying to come up with that great creative idea for writing or illustrating.
- Introduce the M-M strategy by suggesting that sometimes just a single minute of silent mind-searching will result in a good idea.
- Explain how to let the mind wander and fantasize, then practise for a minute. Some possible comments to share with students include these:

  "What happens when you daydream?"
  (You think of many different topics at a time or get fully immersed in one.)
  "If you close your eyes and try to think of nothing, what happens?"
  (The mind "wanders" and grasps at a variety of thoughts.)
  "To allow your mind to wander, breathe deeply, close your eyes if you want to, and just think of anything and everything. Let one thought flow into another. For example, I might be thinking of the sun, which makes me think of summer holidays, which makes me think of eating ice cream. . . ."

- Encourage kids to use the M-M strategy several times.

C-O-O

**Connecting
Opposite
Objects**

Purpose: The C-O-O strategy helps kids to be as creative as possible. It invites them to put together things, ideas, or concepts that wouldn't normally go together. Making those connections means thinking wildly and wonderfully, then using the results in some creative endeavor, such as writing or illustrating. Even a class discussion about unusual connections can stimulate creativity and serve as a worthwhile communication activity.

Strategy Display

1. Make a list of at least five sets of opposites. Possibilities include happy/sad, black/white, in/out, and oil and water (items with resisting properties).

2. Select your favorites and imagine how to make the opposites work, function, or exist together. There are no right or wrong answers. Creativity is the key! Here are examples of how happy/sad might work together:

> Happiness is such a good or high feeling that when it goes, sadness might take its place. The person feels sad because he is no longer happy. Happiness is related to sadness according to the degree of sadness experienced. If one is already very sad, or melancholy, a small change in life may produce happiness. That same small change might have no effect on the life of an already happy person.
> Third World children live in unhappy conditions, but may appear happy when given a small meal.
> A frog in a teacher's desk may make a student happy, but the teacher sad.

Quick Tips

- Discuss the idea of opposites, such as oil and water.
- With older students, you may want to introduce the term *oxymoron*. An oxymoron is an expression with contradictory words, usually put together for effect. The oxymoron "jumbo shrimp" may be common to students: this fits the C-O-O strategy if it can be shown why some shrimp — "shrimp" refers to something very small — might be called "jumbo" (big in relation to other shrimp). Let students brainstorm for oxymorons.
- Discuss how opposites can possibly work together: "How could we get oil and water to mix?" In most cases, there are no logical answers so encourage imaginative thought. The object is creative thinking.

For the "oil and water together" idea, a Grade 4 boy suggested "freeze the water and put a chunk of ice on the oil." Creative!

Solving Problems Innovatively

Problem: **Sometimes, kids get really bogged down when trying to think of alternative or new ways to reach a destination or solve a problem. They can't think creatively because they are stuck in the present, metaphorically unable to reach into the unknown.**

K-C-A-B

Purpose: The K-C-A-B strategy provides an amusing hint to kids to work backwards from an ideal goal or outcome in order to see different steps forward. It helps to answer the "why" question in problem solving.

"BACK"
spelled backwards

The idea of working backwards can be applied to situations such as figuring out the steps in mathematical problems or science experiments when the final answer is supplied, determining possible motivations of story characters when the climax is known, or seeking possible causes of problems in student's own lives.

Strategy Display

1. Start at an end point, perhaps the outcome of a science experiment or the end of a story, and begin taking steps backwards. Find a relevant action that has led directly to the final point, something that has occurred just prior to the "end."
2. Record the step you determined to be closest to the end point. Be creative. If you are using the K-C-A-B strategy with a story, don't write down what you already know happened. Instead, create a new step that would have led to the same outcome.

3. Write down the step, action, activity, or situation that might have come directly before the step already identified, and continue in this manner until you reach the beginning.

Quick Tips

- Be sure to encourage wild and wonderful ideas.
- You may want to begin by playing the Jeopardy game where you provide an answer and ask the students for possible questions. You can then point out how this is an example of the K-C-A-B strategy and a good way to review facts.
- After playing Jeopardy, invite students to figure out the meaning of K-C-A-B.
- Together, practise the K-C-A-B strategy using a familiar story, but creating a different backwards sequence of incidents leading to the same ending.

Problem: Sometimes, students forget that there are many resources to help them solve problems, not the least of which is qualified adults.

ATE

Purpose: The ATE strategy invites kids to think of what an expert would do with the situation, problem, or concern being pondered.

Strategy Display

With the ATE strategy you "give your head a shake" and pretend to be someone else.

1. Imagine you ate something that changed you into another person — an Expert in the area on which you are focusing.
2. Think of questions you would like to ask the expert (assuming the expert was right there with you).
3. Now, eat the imaginary "something" that changes you into the expert, and ask your questions.
4. Answer the questions to the best of your ability as the expert. Remember: this is a task to further creativity — there are no wrong answers!
5. Use your answers for writing, illustrating, discussing, and more.

Quick Tips

- For this highly creative strategy, encourage kids to first create good questions that they want to ask the expert, then to be the experts and answer the questions.
- You might want to connect the idea of eating something magical that turns them into experts with the name of the strategy: ATE.
- It is a good idea to first try the ATE strategy in pairs, but be sure to explain how and where this strategy might be used in real life. For example, you could use it when you are all alone and need to figure out
  how to find a route on a map
  how to follow a recipe
  how to use a guide (e.g., television and theatre listings in newspaper)
  how to create a new dance move

Kids love this strategy and it really taps into their creativity. It is fun to first use it in small groups or pairs.

Ask
The
Expert

Tapping into Inner Creativity

Problem: **Often, students' self-images are skewed, whether by ignorance or choice. They don't quite know who they are or what they really look like and are decidedly uncreative when it comes to describing themselves. They need to tap into their inner creativity to really see themselves.**

MA-B-ME

Purpose: The MA-B-Me strategy invites kids to tap into one of the easiest ways to be creative: to fantasize about themselves and write about "maybe me."

MA
B
Me

The intrinsic fun in this strategy, which lets students guess who's who, masks the fact that they are being creative.

Strategy Display

1. Make a list of your personal qualities, both physical and emotional. This is the Me part of the MA-B-Me strategy.
2. Now, make another list of traits you do not have, but wish you had. This is the MA-B part of the MA-B-Me strategy.
3. Put both lists together in some format, such as an illustration, a graphic organizer, or a piece of writing. Do not put your name on the front of the representation.
4. Add your finished project to all the rest in the class.
5. With the teacher's help, discuss each project and determine the "real me." The teacher pulls one project at a time and leads a class discussion about the person it represents. Only positive traits should be discussed, so the teacher specifically draws attention to these on each representation. Guess the creator of each project, but don't spend more than two or three minutes doing it.
6. Once the creator is correctly identified, connect the Me to the *maybe* parts in this way.

   a) [Student's name] is . . .
   List the Me facts depicted by the representation.
   Consider: "Are there other traits we think this person might have in the future?"
   (The student who is the subject of discussion thereby gains additional suggestions from peers.)

   b) Look at the MA-B section to fill in the next part.
   [name] would like to be . . .
   Ask: "How is this person already like that? What suggests that this person will be . . . some day?"

   c) Ask: "What positive traits did [name] miss on this representation?"

Quick Tips

After the class activity, students may wish to put both parts of the MA-B-Me strategy together into a good piece of writing or a personal poster. Or, they may wish to record in their journals anything they discovered about themselves or others from using the MA-B-Me strategy.

- Use the MA-B-Me strategy as an individual and then as a whole-class activity.
- Always keep comments positive. Discussing how to use positive comments about others may be useful. (Doing this is often a Health topic and may just have to be recalled.)
- Discuss the meaning of the MA-B-Me name.
- Using a personal example is recommended: "I am a teacher. I am also a speed skater. I would like to be a famous speed skater and win a race. On

my representation, I would show myself with a medal." Invite comments. If students are reluctant to tell you that winning a race would not likely happen, ask them outright, but encourage them to answer positively. Someone might say: "You could practise lots and probably do well. You enjoy skating and that's what's important."

- Point out where students could use this strategy in real life. For example, when completing job applications, they could think of the MA-B as what they wish to get from a position and the Me as the accurate description of themselves at that time. Prompt kids to think of other uses.

7

Living Well

Living well means taking, wherever possible, proactive measures to prevent emotional and physical threats to well-being. It is an integrated approach towards the common goal of happiness and health, a balance between mind and body that results in "feeling good." Within the scope of that integrated approach are found stress management, anger management, physical fitness, healthy eating, and positive interactions with others. The assumption of this book is that teachers can help students in pursuit of all of these positive attributes by teaching them strategies for living well.

Why should teachers give precious in-class time to the teaching of living well strategies? The most obvious answer is that if kids are not "living well," they will not accessible to teaching, so considerable class time will be lost. We must also remember that we are instructing our students "for life." Many of the strategies they learn in school will stay with them forever, so let's get them *well* started living *well*.

Teacher will agree that one of the biggest threats to in-class wellness is stress, both the stress of kids and the stress of teachers. Although we all talk about it, no one seems quite sure what it is or what to do about it. It's true that some situations in life are stress provoking, but not all of these are negative. In other words, some stress is *good* stress. The other kind of stress — *dis*tress — is what the strategies offered in this chapter address.

Negative stress is a direct result of the way we *think* about, or *perceive*, a stressful situation. If we believe we have effective coping strategies in place, the situation is deemed less stressful; if we believe our coping strategies are non-existent or weak, the stress grows in strength. By teaching students coping strategies, as those offered here, we are effectively weakening the negative effects of a stressful situation.

Similarly, the teaching of anger management strategies helps kids deal more effectively with this strong emotion. As all teachers know only too well, anger in the classroom can manifest itself in ways ranging from mild irritation to aggressive, acting-out rage. They also know that anger not appropriately dealt with can cause myriad other problems, both physical and emotional. Consequently, as educators we should teach our students how to deal with anger; one effective way to do this is to provide strategy instruction specifically for managing anger.

The other areas in this chapter, although given less weight, are no less important to living well. In order to live well, children must accept themselves and know how to interact with others and with the environment. They must be able to deal effectively with negatives, seek positives, and generally do what is best for themselves within the confines of the culture. Teachers can help with this by sharing appropriate strategies, such as those offered in this chapter.

Dealing with Anger

Problem: **Kids often feel acute anger or frustration, but unlike adults, they haven't developed ways to deal with or conceal these untoward emotions. Our society frowns upon open displays of anger — especially in the classroom. Nevertheless, students often experience this emotion. They tend to keep anger, frustration, and other upsetting feelings simmering near the surface and don't know how to deal with them appropriately, to "let them go" or defuse them.**

P-T-O

Personal
Time **Out**

Purpose: P-T-O teaches students to take time away from a source of annoyance in order to cool down.

Strategy Display

1. When you are feeling angry, or when you think you might get angry, stop what you are doing and take a breath.
2. Next, quietly remove yourself from the situation (the room, the person, the task). Step away. Perhaps go outside or to a different room.
3. Stay there for as long as it takes for your "calm" to return. The time is usually 5 to 10 minutes. While in the Personal Time Out, think calming thoughts, maybe about a beautiful place or about a favorite pet.
4. Return to where you were with a different attitude.
5. Some time that same day, journal the P-T-O. Explain why it was necessary, how you handled it, what you felt, and so on.

Quick Tips

- Discuss the importance of dealing with anger before it escalates.
- Discuss where kids in class can go for a Personal Time Out.
- Establish an appropriate maximum time for a Personal Time Out.
- Disclose when you have used this strategy effectively.
- Discuss the importance of writing about feelings in a journal *after* a Personal Time Out. (Kids will find this cathartic. It helps them better understand their emotions and how to handle them.)

P-A-A

Put
Anger
Away

Purpose: The P-A-A strategy suggests a way to put the anger off until later in a manner that doesn't disavow the emotion, but rather allows that "this is not the time" to express it.

Strategy Display

1. Faced with anger, stop everything, breathe, and say to yourself: "I will deal with this later."
2. Think of a time when you can deal with the anger. It may be as you walk home from school or are alone in your bedroom. Give yourself permission to feel "really mad" at that time.

3. At the pre-chosen time, think about what made you angry. Try to revisit the negative emotions. They will be less powerful then, and you can figure out a way to deal with the situation should it occur again.
4. Reward yourself for using P-A-A. For example, you may wish to give yourself a little treat, such as a candy bar or piece of fruit; an extra five minutes on the phone; a checkmark on the calendar; or a comment in your journal to remind you of your success.

Quick Tips

- Discuss what happens when we get really angry. What are our physical and emotional reactions?
- Discuss poor as opposed to more appropriate times and places for displays of anger.
- Talk about what happens if we never deal with the anger.
- Discuss how to revisit anger at a later time or place.

DOODLEDEE

DoodleDee

Purpose: The DoodleDee strategy is a simple, energy-releasing drawing activity that often brings both relief and insight to the child.

Strategy Display

Feeling angry? Instead of shouting or acting out, grab a pencil and paper and doodle away your anger.

1. Draw a DoodleDee, an evil-looking creature who absorbs all anger.
2. Use heavy, jagged lines that really show your anger.
3. Keep drawing until the anger passes.
4. Congratulate yourself for effectively using DoodleDee.

Quick Tips

- Discuss how "drawing our anger" can be effective.
- Brainstorm on what angry lines and shapes might look like, and what a DoodleDee creature might look like.
- Point out that if kids find themselves in a situation where they don't have pencil and paper, they can draw a DoodleDee in their mind's eye.

RAGE PAGE

**Rage
Page**

Purpose: The Rage Page strategy encourages kids to become involved in what we, as adults, know as a constructive way to deal with anger: to write about it.

Strategy Display

1. Turn to a previously established Rage Page. This page can be a separate sheet or at the back of any scribbler in use.
2. Start writing without planning. Simply let the anger flow onto the page. Avoid trying to problem-solve or analyze the anger at this time. Just write how you feel. Illustrate if you want to.
3. Continue writing or drawing for at least two minutes. Check the room clock as you begin.

Quick Tips

- Discuss free writing as the constant, uninterrupted flow of thoughts on a page.
- Invite each student to find a place for possible Rage Pages. Ask if they want to have a separate scribbler or a box of lined paper readily available.
- Allow all kids to free-write about *anything* while you time them for two minutes. They need to get the "feel" of how much time this is.
- If a student has chosen to use a Rage Page in class, avoid drawing the class's attention to this. Discuss this with the student at a later time, providing positive reinforcement for appropriate behavior.

Coping with Stress and Worry

Problem: **Everyone faces stress. With stress comes worry and anxiety. Kids, however, often jump head first into the stress-provoking situation with either a fight-or-flight approach, neither of which is conducive to problem solving.**

TAKE-5

Purpose: The Take-5 strategy is a reminder to breathe deeply before reacting when under stress. It is used readily by most adults, but not so much by young people. Simply telling young people to breathe deeply is not as effective as teaching them this strategy.

Strategy Display

1. When you first find yourself in a stressful situation, "freeze" physically and mentally.
2. Breathe in deeply through your nose for a count of 5. As you breathe in, your abdomen moves outward and your rib cage moves up and out.
3. Hold that breath with eyes closed for a count of 5.
4. Exhale slowly out of your mouth to a count of 5. As you exhale, your belly button pulls in to your spine and your rib cage moves down towards your hips.
5. With your eyes closed, keep your lungs empty for a count of 5.
6. Repeat up to five times or until you feel calmer.

If you find it difficult to use a 5-count, try a 3-count and gradually increase your ability to slow-breathe up to the 5-count.

Quick Tips

- Discuss stressful situations and how we react to them.
- Discuss and practise the freeze technique. Invite kids to move around in their desks and freeze on cue.
- Teach kids how to "yoga" breathe. They breathe in deeply, making their bellies move *out* as they breathe in and sucking their bellies *in* as they breathe out.
- Practise the five second in-hold-out-hold technique. Encourage closed eyes, if not for the entire process, at least for the "breath-holding" parts.

This form of concentrated breathing may seem backwards, but insist on kids trying to do it. Not only does it use more lung capacity, but the mental focus is also important.

PIGGLE-WIGGLE

Purpose: Piggle-Wiggle involves consciously and forcefully wiggling the toes either in or out of shoes — a deliberate action that helps block anxious thoughts.

Strategy Display

Possibly due to the sheer foolishness of its execution, this amusing strategy is a favorite with many kids. I recall an adult friend sharing that she used Piggle-Wiggle while in the dentist chair as she was so nervous about being there. She found it helped. This strategy kids can take with them forever.

Sixty seconds is a long time — try it!

1. As soon as you realize that you are feeling stress or anxiety, focus on your toes.
2. Try to "see" each toe as you wiggle them as hard as possible for as long as 60 seconds.
3. Stop and revisit the stress-provoking situation. If it is still as worrying, wiggle again.

Quick Tips

- Begin by brainstorming situations that may be stressful.
- Discuss and practise the Piggle-Wiggle strategy, first with shoes off (so kids can really *see* their toes in action) and then with shoes on.

3R-3S

Purpose: The 3R-3S strategy provides kids with concrete actions to take when they are feeling the negative effects of stress.

Strategy Display

Remove Relax Realistic Small Something Sleep

Often, simply knowing how to use this strategy relieves stress.

1. Remove yourself from the stressful situation.
2. Relax by taking a few deep breaths and focusing on the breathing, in and out, in and out.
3. Set a Realistic goal for yourself related specifically to the stressful situation.
4. Don't sweat the Small stuff.
5. Do Something for someone else.
6. Sleep. Be sure to get enough of this.

Quick Tips

- Discuss the idea that everyone feels stress and that sometimes, stress can be helpful. At other times, however, it causes "distress" and in those instances the 3R-3S strategy is useful.
- Share the following with reference to each of the preceding steps:

  Remove: You can either physically move away from something or mentally do so by thinking of something else.
  Relax: Visualize your lungs puffing out and collapsing in with each breath.
  Realistic: Consider the situation and think of a possible "way out." (If the stressor is an upcoming exam, decide what you need to do to pass it; if the stressor is a person, decide what the minimum contact you can handle might be.)
  Small: Remember the saying "Pick your battles." This idea is so true when it comes to situations that cause stress. Seriously consider if it's a small battle. If it is, let it go. Consider it not worth your time.

Something: By focusing on another person, your stressor loses power. There is always someone else who needs your help.

Sleep: Fatigue makes every stressor seem so much worse, so try to get enough sleep at night. If you know you are tired, tell yourself that the situation is being affected by that; plan to revisit the situation when you've had more rest.

CAN-I

Change Accept Negotiate
I

Purpose: The CAN-I strategy reminds kids of three powerful ways to deal with stress and worry, together with the idea that they ("I") have control over the situation. Sometimes, just an awareness of the strategy provides the bit of security needed to deal with the situation.

Strategy Display

Change: Ask yourself if you can change the existing situation. Or, can you change part of it? If so, what part? ("Can **I** change it, if so, how?") If you can change it, you have a focus. If you can't change it, consider the next option.

Accept: Ask yourself if you can accept the situation or any part of it. ("Can **I** accept this?") If you can, you have a focus. If you can't accept it, or can accept only part of it, consider the next option.

Negotiate: Ask yourself how you can negotiate a change in the situation to make it more acceptable to you. ("How can **I** make this easier to bear?") With whom will you negotiate, and how will you negotiate?

Quick Tips

- Discuss how worrying about something is really a waste of time. (However, recognize how difficult it is for kids *not* to worry.)
- Point out that sometimes just taking some sort of action helps alleviate worry.
- Do the CAN-I strategy together using a fictitious situation, such as notification of a huge, mandatory, very difficult exam today.

***Problem:* Insomnia seems to be a growing problem among our students of all ages. Faced with sleeplessness, they become agitated and frustrated.**

REST

Read
Easy
Suppress
Time-out

Purpose: The REST strategy provides kids with a concrete plan of action for times when they are faced with sleeplessness. By having a strategy to employ, the anxiety associated with insomnia is immediately reduced.

Strategy Display

Allow yourself one or two hours. If you are still not sleeping, then employ the REST strategy.

1. First get up and Read something frivolous or unimportant, but interesting (maybe a novel, a comic book).
2. During the reading, focus on Easy breathing; take a deep breath and hold for five seconds, then release slowly. Repeat the Easy breaths three times, then continue reading.

3. Suppress (hold back, control, attempt to block out) any feelings of upset at being awake. Instead, tell yourself it's OK to be awake and reading for a while.
4. Think of this as a Time-out from sleeping. Remember that Time-outs are useful periods of escape from a troubling situation. A Time-out is both positive and rewarding.
5. After using the REST strategy for about 15 to 30 minutes, return to bed. If you still can't sleep, repeat the steps again, reminding yourself that sleep will come eventually.

Quick Tips

- Invite discussion about sleep problems. No doubt, most kids will be able to share personal experiences.
- Assure them that not sleeping sometimes is perfectly normal, but that they can try the REST strategy.

Avoiding the Feeling of Being Overwhelmed

Problem: **Kids, like many adults, can feel overwhelmed by having too much to handle. This feeling of disorganization and of not being in control often leads to anxiety or emotional breakdown.**

PORT

Purpose: The PORT strategy reminds kids that developing and carrying out an effective time management plan is strongly recommended, especially when they are faced with a variety of expectations on their time.

Power
Of
Routine
Time

Students need to know how important it is to establish and stick to a routine, and to avoid impulsive actions. There is great power in routine.

Strategy Display

1. Begin by listing everything that is required of you daily, for a week at a time. Don't forget to plan for "play time" or downtime too.
2. Use an organizer, workbook, or write-on calendar, and work out a daily schedule. If time expectations overlap, you must make a tough decision to prioritize and "let something go" (no, not homework!). If necessary, get help with this stage of routine establishment if necessary.
3. Choose a day to begin sticking to your timetable and be rigid about adhering to it. Give yourself a check or an asterisk (*) for each day of successful use of routine time.

Quick Tips

- Discuss the concept of a safe port in a storm, connecting the storm (metaphorically) to an overwhelming number of time expectations and the PORT as a safe way to deal with them and still maintain sanity.
- Kids will probably need help when figuring out their timetables. Include parents in this as much as possible. Watch that kids don't take on too much. Be sure that they include personal time.
- Encourage kids to journal feelings related to use of rigid timetables. Ask them to express feelings about the PORT strategy. Ask whether their safe ports have helped them.

MINI-ME G

Purpose: The Mini-Me G strategy is to remind kids of the importance of setting small, or mini, goals rather than huge, unreachable ones.

Strategy Display

1. Think of the final outcome, or goal, you wish to reach or achieve.
2. Break down the overall goal into as many smaller Mini-Me Goals as possible.
3. As each Mini-Me Goal is reached, pay attention to how this has brought you closer to the main goal. You may want to list the Mini-Me-Goals briefly and check each one off as it is accomplished.

Main Goal: Learning to swim
Mini-Me Goals:

- To feel OK with my face in the water
- To float in the water
- To dog-paddle in shallow water
- To dog-paddle in deep (over-my-head) water

After successfully completing any of the Mini-Me Goals, you may take a break from pursuit of the main goal. You are still moving towards reaching it.

Quick Tips

- Discuss the concept of goals with the students.
- Invite them to brainstorm for big goals they have.
- Discuss how the best way to reach those goals is to break them down into smaller goals. You may wish to use the idea of one step at a time here, as this applies to so many areas of learning.
- Introduce the Mini-Me G strategy. Most kids will be familiar with "Mini-Me" from the Mike Myers movies, so you can capitalize on that information when introducing this strategy. If they are not familiar, introduce Mini-Me G by asking who they are "mini" to (parents) and who is "mini" to them (younger siblings).
- Invite kids to think of a huge real or imaginary life goal, and to use the Mini-Me G strategy to break it down into as many small, manageable goals as possible. Consider having kids first do this in pairs.
- Talk about how students can reinforce themselves for successfully completing the Mini-Me goals.

Problem: **Kids are often faced with an anxious or upset friend or family member, and may not know how to handle the situation; consequently, the negative feelings may be passed on to them, rather than effectively dealt with.**

CALM

Purpose: The CALM strategy provides kids with concrete steps for dealing with the upset or unhappy feelings of another, thereby allowing them to avoid being caught up in feelings of discomfort.

Strategy Display

Care is shown first by making eye contact and completely "being there" for the other person. Give your full attention.
Accept whatever the person says, without judging. You do not have to agree, but avoid condemning or making a verdict.
Listen carefully to what is being shared and watch for non-verbal cues.
Mentor. Offer support and guide the person towards a possible plan of action.

Quick Tips

- There are many teaching approaches to helping kids help each other. With the CALM strategy, kids must practise all the steps in a non-threatening situation, namely, in class with peers.
- Begin by prompting kids to think of a time when they were faced with an upset peer, family member, or friend, and ask what they did.
- Discuss the CALM strategy and point out how it is useful. (If you follow it immediately, you won't worry that what you are saying or doing is right.)
- As a class, come up with non-judgmental statements, such as those offered below. Encourage use of noncommittal words, such as "maybe, think, perhaps, possibly, sense, imagine." You may wish to share possible scenarios with the students, for example, when you get home from school your mom seems upset or your best friend calls, but is shouting on the phone. Invite students to try to use some appropriate statements. Suggestions include the following:

  I understand what you are saying, even if I don't quite agree with . . .
  I think you mean . . .
  I can tell that you are really upset. I would be too.
  That is a tough situation. I don't have a solution, but let's talk about it and maybe we can come up with some ideas.
  You are in a bad place right now. I *think* I understand how you must feel but I've never had that experience myself.

Taking a Positive Approach

Problem: Kids often get so bogged down with the realities of daily living — school, homework, chores, sibling rivalry — that they neglect to see the beauty around them. They lose sight of what they have to be grateful for. They forget to "look" for the good stuff.

SARI

Purpose: This strategy encourages kids to think of the beauty in a sari from the Indian subcontinent and use this concept of beauty in color and movement to look at familiar, everyday surroundings with appreciation.

See
A
Rainbow
In it

Strategy Display

1. Close your eyes for a moment. Picture a beautiful, multi-colored, flowing, silk sari. See the rainbow of color shimmering before you.
2. Open your eyes. Look around and locate something in the environment that is also beautiful, colorful, or full of movement. Be thankful for being witness to that beauty.

3. Immediately, think of one more item, situation, animal, or person for which you are thankful. Think of this as "looking for a rainbow" every day.

Quick Tips

- Talk about saris. If possible, share a picture or even a real example. Discuss the color and beauty of the garment.
- Compare the color(s) to the colors in a rainbow. (The sheen of a silk sari is such that it can often take on subtly different colors.)
- Connect the name of this strategy, SARI, to the idea of seeing beauty in simple things.
- Discuss being grateful for little things of beauty. Encourage students to frequently make positive comments on what they are thankful for. Model this behavior by sharing with the class something you appreciate: "Every day on the way to school, I pass by Mrs. Smith's front garden. I love the pink roses."
- Discuss situations when the SARI strategy could be useful. Examples include these:
    when you feel lonely or depressed
    when something has gone wrong
    when you have lost something important to you
    when you feel sorry for yourself

Problem: Kids may not realize that everyone experiences similar feelings and ups and downs daily. They think the "terrible feeling" will last forever, and frequently are unaware that there are strategies to help with realistic visualization of mood swings.

FAD

Purpose: This strategy draws kids' attention to how quickly feelings can change, as well as to what possible pitfalls, or things that trigger "bad" feelings, occur during a regular day.

Strategy Display

At the end of a day you will have a visual representation of your mood swings.

1. Draw a horizontal line halfway down a page, starting at one side and ending at the other (midline).
2. Put a plus sign (+) above the line at the farthest left; put a minus sign (–) below the line directly under the plus sign.
3. At intervals throughout the day, put a dot on, over, or below the line to indicate how you are feeling at that time. Concisely "label" the dot, or give the reason for its presence. For example, a student might put a dot slightly below the line because a returned test mark was low, put a dot on the line when no high or low feelings were attached to a story read aloud, put a dot far above the line because physical education was enjoyed, and put a dot far below midline when recess was cancelled due to rain.
4. Draw a vertical line from the dot to the midline; put the time of that recording on the midline.

Feeling
A
Day

I once heard a Grade 6 girl saying to a friend: "Let's each do a FAD today and compare them after school." It made me smile to see how they had internalized this helpful strategy.

Quick Tips

- Discuss what a fad is and how this might connect to the FAD strategy. (The strategy is a good thing to do right now — a "fad," so to speak.)
- Discuss "midline" feelings as being neither high nor low.
- Discuss situations that might trigger high or low feelings. Invite kids to share and compare.
- Point out that no two graphs will look the same; nor should they.
- Discuss how often students may want to mark their FAD graphs. If nothing much happens to produce mood swings, fewer dots would be put on the midline. If, however, a day is filled with ups and downs, there may be many dots.
- For the initial experience, identify specific moments for kids to mark their FAD graphs. Attempt to choose moments in the day when you suspect feelings will be extreme, for example, just before a test or just following a video excerpt.
- Invite kids to keep their FAD graphs and use them for creative writing projects later.

Problem: **Sometimes, life seems unfair; things are just "wrong" and the result is acute or worse still, chronic despair, upset, and maybe even depression. It is a "bad" day!**

SWIM

Purpose: The SWIM strategy capitalizes on the familiar "Sink or swim" adage. It draws attention to the positive results of choosing to swim.

Strategy Display

Smile
Walk
Indulge
Make

Recognize that you are in need of an anxiety-reducing strategy.
1. Find a mirror and Smile at yourself.
2. Go for a brisk Walk, indoors or out, for about 15 minutes.
3. Indulge yourself by doing something you love to do. (Read a comic, listen to music, talk on the phone to a friend, write, draw, or paint.)
4. Now consciously Make someone else smile. Doing this serves a dual purpose. It makes you feel good and helps someone else, too.

"Indulge" can refer to eating or drinking something as long as it is a healthy something, such as a glass of chocolate milk or an apple, and not a fat or sugar-laden something. The latter will cause only a spike in blood sugar and will not help anyone to lose the negative feelings for more than a few moments.

Quick Tips

- Discuss the adage "Sink or swim."
- Discuss having a day when just about everything seems to go wrong. Invite kids to share examples.
- Tie the bad day ideas to sinking. Suggest it might be possible to "swim" on those days too.
- Practise the options of the SWIM strategy together.
- Remind kids that they have a choice: to sink or to swim.

Problem: **All of us, at times, face having to do something we don't want to do. Kids in this situation can find many reasons to avoid the task and even more reasons to complain while doing it.**

DOUBLE P

Purpose: The Double P strategy provides kids with a positive tool for dealing with those dreaded "I-don't-want-to-do-that" situations: these may include doing chores or homework, or even visiting relatives — if problematic, a teenager may wish to negotiate with parents.

Strategy Display

Use your own Personal Power by following these steps.

1. Realize you have little or no choice in the matter and stop complaining.
2. Tell yourself it's only for a set time and that you have the Personal Power to do anything when the end is in sight — establishing the "end" of time spent on this task is important.
3. Use the energy you might have been using to avoid or complain to get at the task immediately.
4. Decide on a personal reward for completing the task. You might want to eat or drink something you like, watch a favorite TV show, listen to a CD, or call a friend. Do not, at any costs, allow yourself this reward until the task or time duration is over. (Some tasks may require several "sittings"; for these, reward yourself after each time period is completed.)
5. Remind yourself that you have Personal Power and can make the task better or worse, easier or more difficult, depending on how you use it.

Quick Tips

- Discuss with kids what sorts of tasks are distasteful to them. Disclose tasks you dislike as well.
- Discuss what we do to avoid doing these tasks — for example, procrastinate — and what the result(s) of these tactics are.
- Talk about the Double P strategy steps together. The most important point is to get kids to agree that they can do anything if an end is in sight.
- Discuss how they can see ahead and establish "ends" to time spent on disliked tasks. Help them to understand what might be an unrealistic "end" (e.g., three hours spent on studying).

PIT

Promised
Individual
Time

I use this strategy all the time, as, I'm sure, do many of you.

Purpose: The PIT strategy is a simple, quick tool for self-reinforcement after a distasteful task has been completed.

Strategy Display

When faced with something you don't want to do, don't let yourself fall into a *pit* by avoiding the task. Use the PIT strategy as follows.

1. Tell yourself you will work at the task for a certain number of minutes (if possible, no more than 30 at a time).
2. At the end of that time, allow yourself so many minutes (about 10 usually) to do something you really like.
3. Stick to your plan and the Promised Individual Time will be even more enjoyable because you will have "earned" it.

Quick Tips

- Discuss doing distasteful tasks, and how hard that can be.
- Disclose a few such personal (but not too personal) tasks with the students.
- Introduce the idea of people "digging themselves into a pit" by avoiding those tasks until they become overwhelming (and they can't get out of the pit).
- Introduce the PIT strategy and brainstorm for possible activities for the reinforcement component.

Looking After Self

Problem: **With today's concerns about poor nutrition and obesity in children, it can be assumed that many students are unaware of exactly what they are putting in their mouths.**

REAL

**Read
Every
Attached
Label**

Purpose: The REAL strategy shows students how to determine what is *real* about foods by encouraging routine examination of labels. It draws attention to food content.

Strategy Display

1. Check the labels of commonly consumed foods, such as cereal, milk products, or canned foods.
2. Look particularly for sodium (salt), fat, and calories.
3. If specific foods do not fit with what you know to be healthy, eat less of them or even avoid them.

Quick Tips

- Bring a few common foods to class. If possible, photocopy the labels and make overheads for whole-class examination.
- Discuss food content and connect to Health lessons about good eating habits.
- Remind kids to apply the REAL strategy often at home.

Problem: **Some kids don't follow the rules of healthy living, including diet, exercise, and rest. In many cases, they are unaware of what's good for them or have forgotten this information.**

MR. FAT

**My Reward
For Aerobics Today**

Purpose: The MR. FAT strategy is an appealing way to remind kids about the importance of daily exercise, in particular, exercise that stimulates the cardio-vascular system — that makes them sweat.

Strategy Display

1. Make a list of all the activities you do that you think could be aerobic.
2. Determine how often you do each.

3. Make a day-plan and list activities that will provide you with about 30 minutes of aerobic exercise daily.
4. Decide how you will reward yourself when you meet the daily requirements (e.g., extra time with an electronic game or a favorite book or comic or TV show, phone call to a friend, special "food" treat providing that calories are not a concern).
5. Keep a checklist and reward yourself each day.

Quick Tips

- Draw attention to the name "MR. FAT" and discuss the strategy.
- Help kids to figure out what aerobic exercise they do daily. (They should be getting at least 30 minutes.)
- Brainstorm with kids how they can meet the requirements and reward themselves.
- Point out how daily exercise helps prevent obesity (*fat* as in MR. FAT).

NEST

Purpose: The NEST strategy is a reminder to kids that they control four areas of their own personal wellness.

Strategy Display

If you want to feel good, you must make positive choices every day about each of the following:

- **Nutrition:** Eat according to the national food guide, at least as much as possible.
- **Exercise:** Daily exercise is a must. Try using the MR. FAT strategy together with the NEST strategy.
- **Sleep:** Try for eight hours per night. Settle for no less than seven.
- **Talk:** Positive self-talk means thinking of the good things, not always the bad. It means being optimistic and cheerful even if things are not going the way you want them to.

If you have made only positive choices during a day, give yourself a simple reward. At bedtime, place a check in the calendar square for that day. After a while, you should be able to see an accumulation of positive choices.

Quick Tips

- Discuss what a nest is — a warm, cozy, safe place — and tie this to the NEST strategy. (If followed, life will be warmer, cozier, and safer.)
- Review the official Food Guide for your country or area.
- Discuss or review the importance of daily exercise. Talk about what sorts of activities "count" as exercise (e.g., walking to school, raking the yard).
- Discuss positive self-talk. Doing this is important. Kids often forget to look for the positives and to remind themselves of what they have to be grateful for.

Nutrition
Exercise
Sleep
Talk

Showing Concern for the Earth

Problem: **Caring for our earth is a topical issue, but sometimes, kids don't realize that their personal contributions are important.**

GREEN

Give
Recycle
Energize
Educate
Note

Purpose: The GREEN strategy reminds kids of steps they can take to help care for our earth and work towards making it greener.

Strategy Display

There are five things people can and should do all the time to work towards a Green earth. Items marked with an asterisk (*) should be done daily.

Give back to the earth by

- helping to plant trees
- protecting ecosystems (don't walk on fragile plants or remove plants or animals)
- carefully picking up and disposing properly of trash and litter*

Recycle bottles, cans, and paper products every day in the correct containers for recycling.*

Energize the earth by conserving energy*:

- Turn off lights.
- Ride a bike or walk rather than travelling by car.
- Watch your water use. You can shower — just not for 20 minutes.
- Turn off entertainment systems, including televisions and computers, when not using them.

Educate others — parents, younger children — about what they can do to help the environment.

Note any serious breaches of good Earth-protecting behaviors (e.g., waste of energy in the school, trash in the schoolyard or neighborhood). Discuss with adults. Consider whether you can play an instrumental role in addressing these problems.

Quick Tips

- It's important that kids become very involved in caring for the environment. The GREEN strategy is a simple and effective way for them to do this. Begin by discussing the name "GREEN" and what that means.
- Invite kids to keep a weekly record of how they specifically follow the GREEN strategy.
- You may wish to have a weekly forum to discuss any concerns they have based on the Note step of the strategy.

Pointing to the Problems

Teachers often encounter the problems outlined below; these problems are directly addressed by strategies in this book.

Chapter 1: Remembering to Learn

Getting Focused

Problem: Kids often "zone out," intentionally or not, when presented with a new learning or when reviewing or studying previously "learned" material. There is a lack of focus on the material to be received. (See page 11.)

Studying and Reviewing

Problem: Some kids are great when it comes to learning and retaining information while in school, but when faced with independent study, they fall short. They don't seem to have the necessary study skills to make their time efficient and effective. (See page 13.)

Committing to Memory

Problem: Some students have more difficulty learning material than others. If they fail to see the relevance or significance of what they are supposed to be learning, it may be impossible for them to remember it. (See page 15.)

Problem: Often, there is more information about a topic than students can recall: they feel overwhelmed by the amount of material. They may remember only sketchy points and be missing chunks of relevant information. Sometimes the "wrong" information is remembered: the irrelevant facts that, in retrospect, are unimportant. Kids will focus on reams of extraneous details about a topic and miss the big picture. Some feel the need to remember everything in order to be good students and end up remembering little. (See page 15.)

Problem: Some people forget information as quickly as it is given. A good example is names. Trying to recall the name of a person, place, or even thing can be enough to drive one crazy. Similarly, some of us can't remember a simple math or science concept as soon as the instruction is over. It's hard for many kids (and many adults) to recall information when it is presented and received only through speaking and listening. (See page 17.)

Problem: All too often, students move on from learning something as soon as they believe they have mastered it. They fail to see the value in "over-learning" — a technique that prompts material to move from short- to long-term memory — and consequently, not be quickly forgotten. (See page 19.)

Problem: Not all memory material comes from the written word. Often, it is necessary to learn and remember graphic detail, such as maps, anatomy, and scientific diagrams. Students trying to memorize pictures or illustrations may experience more difficulty with this than they would with textual material. (See page 21.)

Retrieving Information

Problem: Even after a fact has been "memorized," it can sometimes be difficult to retrieve. This "It's-on-the-tip-of-my-tongue" feeling is something we have all experienced. Kids experience that too, and it can be very frustrating. (See page 22.)

Learning a Procedure

Problem: The whole idea of learning a new procedure fills some kids with anxiety or a sense of not being capable. (Compare this to the way most adults feel when faced with "assembling" a piece of furniture or child's toy, and having to follow instructions to do so.) (See page 23.)

Chapter 2: Communicating

Public Speaking and Talking

Problem: When speaking either formally or informally, students have difficulty getting the point across as they talk around the topic; they are unable to be concise and precise. (See page 25.)

Problem: When getting ready to do an oral presentation of any nature, kids often feel anxious, timid, or uncomfortable. This form of communication can be very intimidating. (See page 26.)

Problem: Sometimes in a discussion, kids repeat what another has just said, over and over again, as if they lack original ideas of their own. (Adults do this, too — it can be very annoying.) This form of communication can be frustrating for everyone involved. (See page 27.)

Problem: Some kids talk with "marbles in their mouths." They slur words, stammer, or enunciate poorly. Clear speaking is a communication survival skill that everyone needs to master. (See page 28.)

Problem: Some people are "boring" to listen to. Their oral communication is flat, monotonous, and uninteresting and consequently fails to attract and maintain attention. (See page 28.)

Problem: Today's kids constantly have to leave voice messages and too often these messages are incomplete or even baffling to the receivers. (See page 30.)

Listening

Problem: Many kids (and adults) do not know how to listen compassionately to their peers' concerns. They fail to respond appropriately, leaving all involved dissatisfied or uncomfortable — a breakdown in communication. (See page 30.)

Problem: Too often, students (and people in general) do not listen actively. This aspect of communication, when it is weak, contributes to many mixed messages and consequent frustrations. (See page 31.)

Persuasion

Problem: Being able to persuade, either in written or oral format, is a necessary life skill not usually perfected by our students. (See page 32.)

Communicating in Writing

Problem: The entire realm of e-mail communication can be problematic for students. It is far too easy to push "Send Now" and immediately wish that the mail could be retrieved. (See page 33.)

Problem: Letter writing, whether via e-mail or snail mail, is an important form of communication at which many kids (as well as many adults) fail to excel. (See page 33.)

Problem: Writing narrative or exposition is one of the most powerful forms of communication — and many of our students struggle terribly with it. They can't seem to get their thoughts on paper and have particular problems when it comes to getting started. (See page 34.)

Problem: Because writing is a valid form of communication, following the rules of good writing is an example of "courtesy" to the reader; however, many kids fail to edit or review their writing. (See page 35.)

Problem: Some kids, often referred to as "apathetic writers," balk at any type of writing. Getting these unmotivated and reluctant students to write can be a monumental task. (See page 35.)

Chapter 3: Organizing

Clearing Out

Problem: An accumulation of "junk" prohibits the finding and using of what is important. (See page 40.)

Organized Ordering

Problem: Often, kids work hard at learning and remembering, only to "forget" much of what they think they have mastered. The cause is often the lack of organization or sequence of presented or studied material. (See page 40.)

Problem: Too often, the cliché "can't see the forest for the trees" describes what happens when students try to organize information for memory. They get swamped by the myriad details and become lost or, at the very least, bogged down. Although this may at first seem like a "memory" problem, it falls under the organization umbrella as it is initially an organizational task. (See page 42.)

Problem: When kids are faced with a writing project, they can feel daunted. Perhaps their ideas are in freefall and they can't get started, or their thoughts are too random, too "large" and unfocused to make writing possible. Getting organized to begin is the problem here. (See page 43.)

Problem: Some kids cannot organize their writing in such a way that they edit. Once written, the piece is considered finished and the idea of returning to it to make changes is seemingly impossible for them. Often, they write too much too quickly, forfeiting accuracy of conventions and clarity of expression. (See page 48.)

Using Graphic Organizers

Problem: Often, reading material is filled with opposing or fluctuating positions, which can make it difficult for students to grasp what is being said. They may experience confusion rather than clarity. This phenomenon can occur, for example, in narratives where a character exhibits a variety of contrary traits or struggles with diverging emotions. (See page 49.)

Making Effective Use of Time

Problem: Time organization can be one of the most daunting issues for students, especially when so many of them are involved in so many areas other than school. (See page 52.)

Chapter 4: Discovering

Expanding Vocabulary

Problem: Many students don't take the time to look up new words or actively increase their spoken and/or written vocabularies. Unless kids are regularly encouraged to expand their vocabularies, many take the easy route and use a dictionary or thesaurus only as needed. (See page 56.)

Exploring Facts

Problem: Although some kids are "turned on" by the discovery of new facts and information, many simply can't be bothered. (See page 56.)

Problem: Kids are expected to use the Internet for discovery — for researching topics and quickly finding information — but often they are overwhelmed by data overload. (See page 57.)

Self-Discovery

Problem: Seeking answers to personal-interest questions is not something most kids do automatically. They may have many queries about themselves, but generally no steps are taken to find answers. This process of self-discovery is lacking. (See page 57.)

Questioning for Information

Problem: When kids don't ask the right questions to get the answers they seek, frustration and tension can be the result and discovery is limited. Knowing how to identify what is needed and then specifically ask for that information is not a built-in skill. (See page 61.)

Problem: It is possible that kids often overlook one of the most important resources for discovery — that of the experience of adults. (See page 62.)

Raising Questions for Deep Understanding

Problem: Students often want to know "more" about a book they are reading. This natural act of discovery may be difficult to capitalize on unless a specific strategy is used. (See page 63.)

Broadening Sources for Discovery

Problem: The Internet is such a huge draw for kids today that many of the other possible sources of information — places that lead to discovery — are overlooked. (See page 64.)

Discovering Truth Through Critiquing

Problem: Kids are faced with so much information that it is often difficult for them to determine what's true and what isn't. The entire area of advertising is a good example. In this case, the presence of inaccurate or biased information, such as that provided by ads featuring overly thin models, can be problematic and frequently confusing. (See page 65.)

Chapter 5: Understanding

Identifying Details

Problem: Students frequently read through an entire passage, but have little idea of what they have read. Frequently, details are overlooked or ignored and there may be confusion as to what information is important and what is not. (See page 68.)

Seeking Answers

Problem: There are many ways to seek answers, to find information, or to satisfy curiosity. Sometimes, students seem bound by the single approach of directly examining the text when other methods would probably be more effective. (See page 69.)

Using Personal Knowledge

Problem: Students read (decode) well, with apparent fluency and ease, but are unable to restate or summarize in their own words what they have read. (See page 71.)

Problem: Students tend to believe explicitly in what they read — in what the words actually say. They often forget to apply their own background knowledge to aid comprehension. (See page 71.)

Problem: Sometimes, kids are unable to grasp what is being presented simply because there seems to be "too much material," and they are unable to put it in context of what they already know and isolate the area of difficulty. (See page 73.)

Figuring Out Narratives

Problem: Sometimes, even after the most enlightening follow-up discussions, it seems students still don't fully understand some specific aspect of a story. It may be something as simple as the motivation of the protagonist or as complex as the author's style of writing. They require an additional strategy for more in-depth comprehension. (See page 75.)

Problem: Following a narrative reading, some kids have trouble reviewing and identifying the key story elements or in understanding exactly what happened, why or how events happened, and what effects these events had on the story. (See page 75.)

Making Sense of Text

Problem: Text can be arranged or structured in so many ways that sometimes students, confused by what they see and perhaps expecting a familiar form, miss important points. They may be unable to sort out what is important from what is less important, and to isolate, paraphrase, or summarize these elements. (See page 81.)

Focusing Attention

Problem: Some kids, often the weaker readers, have considerable difficulty understanding the general content of both narrative and expository text. They struggle with decoding and then struggle even more so with comprehension. They can't focus well enough to tell you what they have "read." (See page 86.)

Chapter 6: Creating

Blasting Mental Blocks

Problem: A major problem faced by kids of all ages is coming up with novel ideas either for writing, speaking, or illustrative purposes. It seems it's all been said or done before. They are left feeling blocked, or "stuck." They don't realize that ideas can come at many different times during the day and be recalled when needed. (See page 90.)

Expanding Existing Ideas

Problem: Students often find it difficult to embellish or make bigger a single idea for creative endeavors. (See page 92.)

Problem: Even the most creative students sometimes forget to use all the possible avenues open to them, the most obvious being their five senses. (See page 96.)

Stepping Away from the Ordinary

Problem: For some kids, it's difficult to "think outside the box," to play what if, to move away from the ordinary, or to escape into fantasy. It seems the older students get, the less able they are to do this. Teachers need to use as many strategies as possible to help students improve their imaginative and creative thinking. (See page 96.)

Solving Problems Innovatively

Problem: Sometimes, kids get really bogged down when trying to think of alternative or new ways to reach a destination or solve a problem. They can't think creatively because they are stuck in the present, metaphorically unable to reach into the unknown. (See page 99.)

Problem: Sometimes, students forget that there are many resources to help them solve problems, not the least of which is qualified adults. (See page 100.)

Tapping into Inner Creativity

Problem: Often, students' self-images are skewed, whether by ignorance or choice. They don't quite know who they are or what they really look like and are decidedly uncreative when it comes to describing themselves. They need to tap into their inner creativity to really see themselves. (See page 101.)

Chapter 7: Living Well

Dealing with Anger

Problem: Kids often feel acute anger or frustration, but unlike adults, they haven't developed ways to deal with or conceal these untoward emotions. Our society frowns upon open displays of anger — especially in the classroom. Nevertheless, students often experience this emotion. They tend to keep anger, frustration, and other upsetting feelings simmering near the surface and don't know how to deal with them appropriately, to "let them go" or defuse them. (See page 104.)

Coping with Stress and Worry

Problem: Everyone faces stress. With stress comes worry and anxiety. Kids, however, often jump head first into the stress-provoking situation with either a fight-or-flight approach, neither of which is conducive to problem solving. (See page 106.)

Problem: Insomnia seems to be a growing problem among our students of all ages. Faced with sleeplessness, they become agitated and frustrated. (See page 108.)

Avoiding the Feeling of Being Overwhelmed

Problem: Kids, like many adults, can feel overwhelmed by having too much to handle. This feeling of disorganization and of not being in control often leads to anxiety or emotional breakdown. (See page 109.)

Problem: Kids are often faced with an anxious or upset friend or family member, and may not know how to handle the situation; consequently, the negative feelings may be passed on to them, rather than effectively dealt with. (See page 110.)

Taking a Positive Approach

Problem: Kids often get so bogged down with the realities of daily living — school, homework, chores, sibling rivalry — that they neglect to see the beauty around them. They lose sight of what they have to be grateful for. They forget to "look" for the good stuff. (See page 111.)

Problem: Kids may not realize that everyone experiences similar feelings and ups and downs daily. They think the "terrible feeling" will last forever, and frequently are unaware that there are strategies to help with realistic visualization of mood swings. (See page 112.)

Problem: Sometimes, life seems unfair; things are just "wrong" and the result is acute or worse still, chronic despair, upset, and maybe even depression. It is a "bad" day! (See page 113.)

Problem: All of us, at times, face having to do something we don't want to do. Kids in this situation can find many reasons to avoid the task and even more reasons to complain while doing it. (See page 113.)

Looking After Self

Problem: With today's concerns about poor nutrition and obesity in children, it can be assumed that many students are unaware of exactly what they are putting in their mouths. (See page 115.)

Problem: Some kids don't follow the rules of healthy living, including diet, exercise, and rest. In many cases, they are unaware of what's good for them or have forgotten this information. (See page 115.)

Showing Concern for the Earth

Problem: Caring for our earth is a topical issue, but sometimes, kids don't realize that their personal contributions are important. (See page 117.)

Index